DATE DUE

JEWEL

OVERCOMING ADVERSITY

JEWEL

John Thompson

Introduction by James Scott Brady,
Trustee, the Center to Prevent Handgun Violence
Vice Chairman, the Brain Injury Foundation

Chelsea House Publishers
Philadelphia

CHELSEA HOUSE PUBLISHERS

EDITOR IN CHIEF Sally Cheney
PRODUCTION MANAGER Pamela Loos
ART DIRECTOR Sara Davis
DIRECTOR OF PHOTOGRAPHY Judy L. Hasday
SENIOR PRODUCTION EDITOR J. Christopher Higgins

Staff for **JEWEL**
SENIOR EDITOR John Ziff
ASSISTANT EDITOR Rob Quinn
ASSOCIATE ART DIRECTOR/DESIGNER Takeshi Takahashi
PICTURE RESEARCHER Sandy Jones
COVER DESIGNER Keith Trego

The Chelsea House World Wide Web address is:
http://www.chelseahouse.com

First Printing

1 3 5 7 9 8 6 4 2

Library of Congress Cataloging-in-Publication Data

Thompson, John.
Jewel / John Thompson.
p. cm. — (Overcoming adversity)
Includes bibliographical references and index.

ISBN 0-7910-5895-6 (alk. paper) — ISBN 0-7910-5896-4 (pbk.: alk. paper)

1. Jewel, 1974-. —Juvenile literature. 2. Rock musicians—United States—Biography—Juvenile literature. [1. Jewel, 1974-. 2. Singers. 3. Women—Biography.] I. Title. II. Series.

ML3930.J49 T56 2001
782.42164'092—dc21
[B]

00-065971

CONTENTS

OVERCOMING ADVERSITY

TIM ALLEN
comedian/performer

MAYA ANGELOU
author

THE APOLLO 13 MISSION
astronauts

LANCE ARMSTRONG
professional cyclist

DREW BARRYMORE
actress

DREW CAREY
comedian/performer

JIM CARREY
comedian/performer

BILL CLINTON
U.S. president

TOM CRUISE
actor

MICHAEL J. FOX
actor

WHOOPI GOLDBERG
comedian/performer

EKATERINA GORDEEVA
figure skater

SCOTT HAMILTON
figure skater

JEWEL
singer and poet

JAMES EARL JONES
actor

QUINCY JONES
musician and producer

ABRAHAM LINCOLN
U.S. president

WILLIAM PENN
Pennsylvania's founder

JACKIE ROBINSON
baseball legend

ROSEANNE
entertainer

MONICA SELES
tennis star

SAMMY SOSA
baseball star

DAVE THOMAS
entrepreneur

SHANIA TWAIN
entertainer

ROBIN WILLIAMS
performer

BRUCE WILLIS
actor

STEVIE WONDER
entertainer

ON FACING ADVERSITY

James Scott Brady

I GUESS IT'S a long way from a Centralia, Illinois, train yard to the George Washington University Hospital Trauma Unit. My dad was a yardmaster for the old Chicago, Burlington & Quincy Railroad. As a child, I used to get to sit in the engineer's lap and imagine what it was like to drive that train. I guess I always have liked being in the "driver's seat."

Years later, however, my interest turned from driving trains to driving campaigns. In 1979, former Texas governor John Connally hired me as a press secretary in his campaign for the American presidency. We lost the Republican primary to a former Hollywood star named Ronald Reagan. But I managed to jump over to the Reagan campaign. When Reagan was elected in 1980, I was "sitting in the catbird seat," as humorist James Thurber would say—poised to be named presidential press secretary. I held that title throughout the eight years of the Reagan administration. But not without one terrible, extended interruption.

It happened barely two months after the Reagan administration took office. I never even heard the shots. On March 30, 1981, my life went blank in an instant. In an attempt to assassinate President Reagan, John Hinckley Jr. armed himself with a "Saturday night special"—a low-quality, $29 pistol—and shot wildly as our presidential entourage exited a Washington hotel. One of the exploding bullets struck me just above the left eye. It shattered into a couple dozen fragments, some of which penetrated my skull and entered my brain.

The next few months of my life were a nightmare of repeated surgery, broken contact with the outside world, and a variety of medical complications. More than once, I was very close to death.

The next few years were filled with frustrating struggles to function with a paralyzed right side, struggles to speak and communicate.

To people who face and defeat daunting obstacles, "ambition" is not becoming wealthy or famous or winning elections or awards. Words like "ambition" and "achievement" and "success" take on very different meanings. The objective is just to live, to wake up every morning. The goals are not lofty; they are very ordinary.

My own heroes are ordinary folks—but they accomplish extraordinary things because they try. My greatest hero is my wife, Sarah. She's accomplished a lot of things in life, but two stand out. The first has been the way she has cared for me and our son since I was shot. A tremendous tragedy and burden was dropped unexpectedly into her life, totally beyond her control and without justification. She could have given up; instead, she focused her energies on preserving our family and returning our lives to normal as much as possible. Week by week, month by month, year by year, she has not reached for the miraculous, just for the normal. Yet in focusing on the normal, she has helped accomplish the miraculous.

Her other most remarkable accomplishment, to me, has been spearheading the effort to keep guns out of the hands of criminals and children in America. Opponents call her a "gun grabber"; I call her a national hero. And I am not alone.

After a seven-year battle, during which Sarah and I worked tirelessly to educate the public about the need for stronger gun laws, the Brady Bill became law in 1993. It was a victory, achieved in the face of tremendous opposition, that now benefits all Americans. From the time the law took effect through fall 1997, background checks had stopped 173,000 criminals and other high-risk purchasers from buying handguns, and the law has helped to reduce illegal gun trafficking.

Sarah was not pursuing fame, or even recognition. She simply started at one point—when our son, Scott, found a loaded handgun on the seat of a pickup truck and, thinking it was a toy, pointed it at Sarah.

Fortunately, no one was hurt. But seeing a gun nearly bring a second tragedy upon our family, Sarah became determined to do whatever she could to prevent senseless death and injury from guns.

Some people think of Sarah as a powerful political force. To me, she's the person who so many times fed me and helped me dress during my long years of recovery.

Overcoming obstacles is part of life, not just for people who are challenged by disabilities, illnesses, or tragedies, but for all people. No matter what the obstacle—fear, disability, prejudice, grief, or a difficulty that isn't likely to "just go away"—we can all work to make this world a better place.

Jewel Kilcher has inspired millions of fans with her music and her unusual life story. The singer-songwriter pursued her dreams in the face of formidable obstacles.

1

ON THE BRINK

LIKE MOST COFFEEHOUSES, the Innerchange in San Diego was a small, intimate place where people gathered to discuss current events and art while listening to open-mike poetry readings or local musicians. Standing-room-only crowds aren't usually found at a place like this. Yet one spring evening in 1993, a young singer named Jewel showed up for her usual Thursday night gig to find a line of people waiting to get in. Confused about all the commotion, she peered through a window to see every available chair occupied by a body. It was so crowded, in fact, that the only way for her to get to the stage was to walk gingerly across the tabletops. She did so to the rousing applause of her fans.

Most people don't recognize a turning point in their life until many years later. Making her way to the stage that night, Jewel was more embarrassed than anything about all the attention. It didn't occur to her that her life had suddenly and permanently changed. No longer was she merely a local surfer girl hanging out and scribbling poetry at the beach, or a transplanted Alaskan farm girl—facets of Jewel's life to that point. She was now *the* musical phenomenon of San Diego, with sold-out gigs, praise coming from the local press, and—unknown to her at the time—hordes of hungry record company agents in Los Angeles looking to sign her to a deal.

But on this night she was still just a 19-year-old folksinger on a tiny stage in a tiny coffeehouse, addressing the crowd as if they were old friends. In fact, most of the faces in the crowd were friends. She'd been performing at the Innerchange for about nine months, but already her Thursday night gigs had won her a loyal following. For many who attended the show, not having a seat was a small price to pay to watch Jewel mix her songs with jokes, stories, a homespun philosophy, youthful energy, beauty, and a magical voice.

After the show most of the audience went home to watch a late movie on TV or snuggle with a loved one in a soft, comfortable bed. But not Jewel. She was homeless.

Homelessness affects millions of Americans. It's a way of life that most people will never understand, and certainly very few would ever willingly adopt. It means no TV, no bathroom, no telephone, no Internet access, no E-mail. Homeless people often have only the clothes on their back. Being homeless means not knowing for sure where the next meal may come from, or if there will be a place to get in out of the rain. It means burning up from the heat in the summer and having no shelter from the freezing cold in the winter. It means being poor. It means being a social outcast.

Yet some people have a special kind of inner strength and willpower that allows them to rise above the depressing circumstances of homelessness and poverty. Such a person is Jewel. But unlike the many desperate people who have become homeless after losing their job or falling into drug or alcohol abuse, Jewel willingly became homeless. She quit a series of dead-end jobs and began living in a van in order to cut costs and pursue a dream. "I was struggling to eat and pay the rent," Jewel said in a newspaper interview, "and when I moved into the van I felt a tremendous relief. I no longer had to come up with $500 a month and I could start being creative."

As positive as that may sound, the decision to become homeless was possibly the lowest point in Jewel's life. After graduating from a performing arts high school in Michigan, Jewel had moved to San Diego to live with her mom, Nedra. Jewel worked as a waitress at various restaurants but had a hard time staying focused on her job. She was more interested in talking to her customers than in taking their orders. She loved finding out about people's lives, listening to their stories and adventures. Jewel drew inspiration and strength from these people. "I don't think I've gone through anything other people haven't gone through," she says. "My feelings are not that original. My expression of them makes them unique. We all have lust, loneliness and insecurity."

It is estimated that up to 2 million people, including 700,000 on any given night, experience homelessness in the United States each year. This homeless person seeks shelter in the doorway of St. Paul's Church in downtown Boston.

But her interest in other people's lives didn't make her a good waitress, because she took so long to serve each customer. She also became frustrated by the amount of time her job took away from her real love: singing and writing. Of course, millions of people feel that the necessity of work keeps them from their true love—whatever that may be. Most choose to be realistic, to keep their steady job and pursue their dreams in their spare time. Jewel chose a different route—but not without much consideration.

Before taking the plunge of living out of her van, Jewel was flooded with doubts. Although she had always been thrifty and wasn't concerned with material success, Jewel worried that in the end she would have nothing to show for her trouble.

Finally she decided that it wasn't worth trying to hold down a regular job. She moved out of her apartment and into her van, which she parked near the beach—one of her favorite places. Jewel felt peaceful at the beach and loved to sit on the sand and write poetry. She could also play guitar and, thanks to having studied voice in high school, was a pretty good singer.

Comfortable performing in front of strangers, Jewel soon began playing at coffeehouses in and around San Diego. A talent like Jewel's doesn't stay local for long, though. "I just got a good word of mouth going," she says. "It was never a goal to make demos for record labels. Word spread somehow to [record companies] in L.A. and then one night someone from Virgin [Records] came down, and this was before I knew the beauty of expense accounts. I bought him a burrito. He told me I could make a record. Then another label came, and another label came. It happened like that."

Such matter-of-factness seems out of place in today's high-profile pop-star world of pretty-boy bands and teenage ingenues. But Jewel often seems out of place in the role of pop star, coming off as a throwback to a simpler time in music history. With her acoustic guitar and lyrics about peace, love, and understanding, Jewel has been compared with folksinger Joni Mitchell. It's a comparison that makes her uncomfortable. "I feel like a pup," says Jewel. "Janis Joplin, Joni Mitchell and Ella Fitzgerald were the real deals."

It's not hard to see Jewel's respect for music history or pick out her influences. She recorded her first album, *Pieces of You,* at Neil Young's private studio, and she has been the opening act for Bob Dylan. Jewel has said that she looks up to artists "who've never lost their creative integrity of what they're doing. . . . It's very rare. The

A star of the late 1960s and early 1970s, Janis Joplin became popular with songs such as "A Piece of My Heart" and "Me and Bobby McGee." Her music was a significant influence on Jewel.

world has become very immediate. It's hard to stay with one's creative drive."

Jewel eventually signed a contract with Atlantic Records. While signifying a new beginning in her life, it also marked the end of a long road of overcoming obstacles, including dyslexia, a broken home, and growing up poor on a farm without electricity or running water. These challenges only made Jewel work harder. "I saw friends on welfare starting to shoplift instead of using their food stamps," she says. "I had a friend, Edward, who was always kind of a fat kid, and he was 18 when he killed himself. Just seeing those levels of humanity touches and bites your heart in a way that you'll never be free from. It made me incredibly determined."

A scene from Homer. Jewel grew up on an 800-acre homestead near the small Alaskan city.

2

A JEWEL IN THE ROUGH

JEWEL'S PATERNAL GRANDPARENTS, Yule and Ruth Kilcher, left their home in Switzerland in 1941 and, having a pioneering spirit, headed for the still-untamed territory of Alaska. There the Kilchers would have a chance to claim large tracts of land and put down roots. They were also drawn to Alaska, which was not unlike their native country, by the stunning beauty of its mountains and fjords. The Kilchers settled just north of the town of Homer, on scenic Kachemak Bay. For all its beauty, however, the Kachemak Bay area can be a harsh place to live. It's rich in natural resources, and the summers bring warm, calm weather. But Alaskan summers are also very short, while long nights and extreme cold characterize the winters.

Yule and Ruth were determined to turn their dreams into reality. Yule cleared land for a farm himself, all by hand. They also had a large family to help with the chores. Jewel's father was the youngest of eight children: Mairiis, Wurtila, Fay, Sunrise, Otto, Stellavera, Catkin, and little Atz.

Yule raised his children the way he had been raised. He was strict and would tolerate no foolishness, yet at the same time he believed that a life without art or beauty was no life at all. Not only did he teach his children to sing, but he also instructed them in skills that had practical as well as artistic value. If you needed something on the farm, you couldn't just go to the nearest mall and buy it. You had to make it. If you wanted a basket to hold potatoes, you wove one out of willow roots. If you wanted a new handle for your ax, you carved one from the limb of an oak tree. And if you wanted entertainment while you went about your chores, you sang or told stories. Music also served as a way to bring the family together and solve conflicts. "Singing was always a big unifying force [in the family], no matter what other conflict went on," says Atz's sister Mairiis "Mossy" Davidson. "You can't be mad at each other when you have to harmonize."

Soon enough the children had grown and were ready to start their own families. Atz married Lenedra Carroll, called Nedra for short, and they had a son named Shane. Jewel was born in May of 1974 in Utah, where Atz and Nedra were attending college. But the family soon moved back to Alaska, and Jewel's younger brother, also named Atz, was born.

Jewel's earliest memories begin with the Kilcher farm in Alaska. Although the beauty and simplicity of life on the 800-acre homestead helped shape Jewel's outlook on life, the rigors of farm living also made her tough. Commenting later on how this upbringing prepared her for the sometimes-difficult life of a touring musician, Jewel said that living on a farm "was a hard discipline, physical labor, lots of chores and not too many luxuries." Not only were there backbreaking chores to be done—feeding animals, hauling hay, harvesting crops—but the basic necessities most people take for granted were absent. There was no electricity or running water—only a coal stove and an outhouse. "There was no TV," Jewel recalls. "Instead, I would sit down and write something."

Yule Kilcher, Jewel's paternal grandfather, believed that a life without art was no life at all.

Jewel and her brothers were taught to pursue other forms of expression as well. For example, Nedra held poetry readings on Mondays, encouraging her children to write and perform their own verses. So while outsiders might think the Kilcher homestead would make for a harsh and monotonous life, it turned out to be a place where the children could develop and thrive. Jewel recalls it as a place of peace and solitude. "I loved being raised there," she says. "There was a lot of silence and open space. In some ways we're sculptured by our environ-

Clouds hang low over the Kachemak Bay. Jewel has called this area, where she spent much of her childhood, the most beautiful place in the world.

ments. Our flesh is sculptured by what is around [us], as well as our psyches."

Like many young girls, Jewel loved animals, especially horses. Living on a farm meant she got to take care of cows, rabbits, dogs, cats, and, of course, horses. Her favorite was called Clearwater, and she shared a special bond with this horse. When he first came to the Kilchers, the horse was very sick, and no one thought he would survive. Among his many problems was his refusal to eat. Jewel's parents tried to keep her from becoming too attached to the horse, fearing that she would take his inevitable death too hard. But the little girl refused to believe that the horse was doomed. Mustering all the will her tiny body could hold, she sat with Clearwater night and day, constantly coaxing and cajoling the animal to eat. Finally, after a long vigil, she succeeded. Clearwater became not just her pet, but her friend, carrying her on many adventures throughout her childhood and easing some of the loneliness of farm life.

Other than crafts and the chores of the farm, Jewel and her brothers didn't have much in the way of entertainment, at least not the sort of entertainment most kids growing up at that time had. Jewel may have been able to tell time by the shadows cast by the sun, but she didn't know anything about the popular sitcoms or teen idols of the day. And not only didn't they have TV or video games, the Kilcher kids didn't even have board games. "A lot of kids grow up knowing how to bank, but I'm [clueless] about city things," Jewel says. "But," she adds with a touch of self-deprecating humor, "I know what a porcupine sounds like climbing a tree."

Living on the farm also taught Jewel about the cycles of life. Instead of learning this through some pamphlet or instructional video, she learned it through natural, everyday occurrences on the farm, where animals were born, mated, and died. "I thought for a long time that it was a negative that I wasn't raised with a lot of outside influences," she says. "I'm beginning to realize that it kept me very creative. I was never taught to watch TV."

Despite the lack of television and other forms of modern media on the farm, Jewel's life wasn't totally without outside influences. When she was five, Jewel picked out a half-price cassette tape of what she thought were songs by the Pink Panther cartoon character. But it was actually *The Wall* from the rock group Pink Floyd. Nevertheless, she listened to that cassette tape until it wore out. This helped develop her taste for music, which would expand to include other classic artists, such as Ella Fitzgerald, Joni Mitchell, and Cole Porter. She found albums by all of these artists and others in her father's record collection.

She also liked songs from the Beatles, even though she didn't know what they looked like—an important factor for many of their young female fans. More than just enjoying the music of the legendary Fitzgerald, Jewel learned to sing just like her, imitating each note, each phrasing—even the way Fitzgerald breathed. As her father once said, "Anything I would tell her to do with her voice, she could do."

Atz and Nedra Kilcher, folksingers who performed at county fairs and run-down roadhouses throughout Alaska, believed in bringing up their kids a bit differently from the *Brady Bunch* image of the '70s. By the time Jewel was six years old, she was going on tour with her parents. "They did sketches and songs," she remembers, "and me and my brothers got up and did numbers."

Spending so much time in such surroundings could have done more harm than good to some youngsters. But Jewel says it enhanced her appreciation of individuals. "Singing in bars, and seeing what goes on in seedy dives from a very young age could have ruined me," Jewel says, "but instead it made me get fascinated by people and want to record people's emotional history, see what motivates us, see what motivates me."

What motivated Jewel at that time, it seems, was performing. Atz and Nedra didn't force Jewel to join them on tour—she wanted to go. Performing with her parents onstage was no game, though. Being able to sing at that level required dedication and hard work. Jewel later recalled that she "used to practice [singing] constantly, mercilessly, learning different harmonies, learning to imitate a lot of different voices." This amount of hard work may sound harsh for a little girl, but Atz and Nedra weren't singing just for something to do. They were, and Atz still is, a vital part of the folk-music scene in Alaska. He and Nedra not only played bars and fairs, but also recorded a couple of albums. And the talent ran in the Kilcher family. Mossy Davidson, Jewel's aunt, was also a popular

Eight-year-old Jewel performs with her father, folksinger Atz Kilcher. An eager student, the young girl was able to use her voice in ways seasoned artists would admire.

Alaskan entertainer with a recording or two under her belt. To perform with her parents, Jewel needed to have her skills up to par.

On top of all the work it took to perform with her parents, Jewel decided on her own to learn to yodel like her father and grandfather. Learning this style of singing is extremely difficult, and Jewel's father didn't think a six-year-old should attempt it. A yodel is basically a way of alternating between falsetto (artificially high) notes and regular notes, and he felt a six-year-old's vocal cords might not be able to handle the strain. Also, it requires concentration and stamina to sustain the yodel for any length of time.

Jewel performs with her mother. Herself an experienced and talented singer, Nedra Carroll Kilcher encouraged her three children to develop their creative gifts.

Undaunted, Jewel began practicing in secret, pushing herself to the limit in order to yodel with her father onstage one day. After many weeks of hard work Jewel surprised her dad with her new skill. Not only had she shown her father that she could do it, but her dedication to succeed on her own impressed him considerably. From then on, she yodeled all she wanted.

No amount of practice or dedication, though, could prevent the biggest tragedy in Jewel's life. When she was eight years old, her parents divorced. Nedra went to live in nearby Anchorage, while Atz and the children remained at the family farm. Although the parents had been granted joint custody of their children, this was the arrangement they felt worked best. Atz and Nedra remained on friendly terms, but the divorce was to have a lasting effect on their young daughter.

When asked about the divorce in later years, Jewel revealed the heartbreak. "It was hard," she said, "and it doesn't matter which parent you lose—as a child it is devastating." Fortunately Jewel and her brothers saw their mother frequently. Most of the time, though, they lived in a converted barn on the homestead. During this rough time Jewel began writing to help her express her feelings.

Hard though it may have been, Atz soon got back to business, and Jewel again joined her father on his singing tours. "When my parents divorced it was just me and my dad," she says. "He taught me professionalism and showmanship. I sang harmony behind him on 'Heartbreak Hotel' and Eagles numbers even though I had never heard the originals." Instead of the folk festivals and fairs where her parents had performed, Jewel and her father played mainly at roadhouses and seedy taverns. Full of drunks, drug addicts, and cigarette smoke, these joints were no place for a sensitive, talented young girl like Jewel. As with every other obstacle in her life, however, she not only learned to overcome it, but also took away some valuable lessons. The most important lesson may have been to steer clear of drugs and alcohol. "There's a lot of darkness I battle in my own mind," she says. "If I were to do drugs or alcohol, it would sink me. . . . I've tortured myself mentally [in the past]—it doesn't feel good."

Not all of the darkness was internal. Because Jewel and her father played in the same bars on a steady basis, she got to know some of the customers pretty well. At one tavern a regular customer who was a veteran of the Vietnam War would lay his money out in ordered piles on the bar.

For the 12-year-old Jewel, Hawaii was no paradise. Wanting to see the world, she went to live with an aunt there, but relentless bullying by local kids spurred her to return to Alaska within a year.

Each night he would sit and drink alone until the money was used up. Halfway through his second pitcher of beer, he would request the same three songs: "Ain't Gonna Study War No More," "Cottonfields," and "House of the Rising Sun." During her breaks Jewel would go sit with the old soldier, who gave her money and let her order sodas or Shirley Temples.

One night, however, he didn't come in. He had been living with too much pain for too long. He was found in his rented room after having shot himself in the head. It turned out he had been a medic in the war and had witnessed the horror that goes along with such a job. Apparently he just couldn't deal with it any longer. "He didn't have any family," Jewel recalls, "so we gave him a fund-raiser to get him a coffin."

But not all gigs were this somber. Atz was more than just a musician; he was a born storyteller and a kind of folksy stand-up comic to boot. Between songs he might recount a funny joke he had heard earlier or tell a story about his younger days in Alaska. Sometimes he would improvise and use the patrons of the bar or tavern as the characters in absurd, sometimes bawdy, adventures. Atz never used a set song list in his act and would even make up songs on the spot just to amuse Jewel or himself. "[My dad] taught me that you can get your brain that loose, just make up words on the spot," says Jewel.

Another good lesson Jewel learned at an early age also took place in a bar. One night, after an argument with her father, Jewel went onstage pouting and defiant. Even though Atz told her to leave her personal life behind when she performed, Jewel continued to sob and pout. Suddenly an old drunk at the front of the crowd yelled to her to stop looking so depressed and get on with the show. In a flash of insight Jewel realized that not only could she entertain these people, she could, perhaps, bring a bit of joy and lightness into their lives. She realized that the performance was for the benefit of the audience, not the performer.

Later in her career, after her first album had gone platinum (sold 1 million copies) and she had branched out into books and movies, Jewel would realize how much this episode had affected her. It was, she recalls, when she first thought about becoming a performer. For Jewel, it would never be about the money and fame, but about having a purpose and helping other people achieve what she calls spirituality. "Spirituality is all aspects of being human," she says. "How do you have courage? How do you love yourself when you don't live up to your own standards? How do you stop feeling bad when feeling bad is all you've ever done?"

When she turned 12, Jewel's spirit drove her to seek out a new adventure. She convinced her parents she needed to see more of the world and went to stay with an aunt who lived in Hawaii. This was a huge change for the young girl and had a profound impact on Jewel's life. If she thought her eccentricities made it hard to live in her native Alaska, Jewel soon found it was almost impossible to live in Hawaii. Caucasians are in the minority in Hawaii, and as a blue-eyed blond with interests that weren't exactly typical, Jewel was often looked down upon—and sometimes even physically attacked—by the locals.

One day as a group of school bullies were about to beat her up, Jewel suddenly began yodeling at the top of her lungs. Stunned, and delighted by the sound, the toughs backed off. But instead of getting better, the bullying got worse. The school bullies began threatening to hurt her if she didn't yodel. Fortunately for Jewel, her stay in the tropics lasted less than a year.

Upon returning to Alaska, Jewel decided to live with her mother in Anchorage rather than return to the farm. Although Jewel continued to perform with Atz whenever he was at a nearby venue, for the most part her life became more like that of a typical teenager. She began to be interested in boys, clothes, and makeup. She even got into a few scrapes with authorities for shoplifting and other juvenile pranks. When Jewel entered the eighth grade, she faced yet another challenge; this time, however, it was a challenge she hadn't searched out. She was diagnosed with dyslexia, a learning disability that affects concentration and reading. But this obstacle only made the tough girl even tougher. Reading and writing were already important parts of how Jewel made sense of her world. They were her solace and a way for her to relax.

She refused to let her disability rob her of something she liked as much as anything else in the world. Instead she vigorously pursued the corrective exercises prescribed and began to read even more to compensate. Attacking trouble head on would become her way of handling difficult situations for the rest of her life. "I think because I'm dyslexic, I always tended to overcompensate," she says. "I have to try things so much harder, I end up trying 20 times harder than I really need to."

It was a work ethic that would serve her well in the coming years.

Jewel broadened her artistic horizons at Interlochen Fine Arts Academy in Michigan, where she completed her junior and senior years of high school. She had won a scholarship to study voice at the prestigious institution.

3

NEW DIRECTIONS

FOR MANY KIDS the junior high and high school years can be a lonely, bewildering time. Those who don't fit in with the rest of the crowd may be ignored or even bullied. Luckily for Jewel, her early teen years weren't as bad as what a lot of kids that age face. But, entering high school, she was still quite different from the rest of her classmates. She had lived on a rustic farm, and she was ignorant of the pop culture her peers swam in. Not having had a computer, a TV, or even a phone, Jewel didn't know anything about popular television comedy series or video games. Plus she was artistic, she didn't follow the fashions of the time, and—worst of all—she yodeled.

Unlike many high school freshmen, Jewel loved to read and eagerly sought out books on philosophy, poetry, and history. Perhaps because of her experience with dyslexia, Jewel was not about to waste the opportunity to enjoy the written word. Among her favorites to read were the philosophers Immanuel Kant, Blaise Pascal, and Plato, and the Latin American poets Pablo Neruda, Octavio Paz, and Gioconda Belli. Jewel was especially attracted to the idea that immortality could be achieved through love and beauty.

For a young person these were powerful ideas. Like most teenagers, Jewel was struggling with her identity, as well as the concepts of life, death, and rebirth. But Jewel had other influences too. Tempering the purely rational philosophy of Kant and Plato were the sensual writings of Henry Miller and Anaïs Nin. From these writers she began to understand that in addition to our spiritual and mental aspects, humans also have bodies with physical needs and desires. These authors also reinforced her belief that love and truth and beauty are also physical things, not just philosophical ideals. "What is truth if it's deducted through pure reason?" Jewel says. "Full truth has to be balanced with emotion and with the living world." She realized that kings and poets and philosophers and rock stars are humans, and as such they are subject to the same emotions and bodily needs all humans feel. They feel loved or unloved, pretty or ugly, smart or stupid; they fall in love, grow old, and die.

These ideas twirled around inside Jewel's head for years, influencing her songwriting and performing, as well as her approach to everyday life. They may have helped prepare her for yet another important life experience that took place when she turned 14. Jewel was formally adopted into a Native American tribe called the Ottawa. Among the sacred ceremonies was one called a "talking circle." Members of the tribe sat in a large circle, and as each individual's turn came up, he or she told a story, sang a song, or perhaps related a dream. From this Jewel learned that although she had filled notebooks with poems and stories, unless she said them out loud—"talked story" as her Ottawa uncle called it—she wasn't doing anyone else any good. Her ideas, thoughts, stories, and poems were her gift to the world, but an object wasn't a gift until it had been given to someone.

Of course, finding a gift and giving it to the world is not such an easy task, especially for a poor, young girl. "I'm

As a teenager, Jewel devoured the works of the Greek philosopher Plato, depicted here teaching a student. Other favorite authors included the Latin American poets Octavio Paz and Pablo Neruda, the sensual writers Henry Miller and Anaïs Nin, and the philosophers Immanuel Kant and Blaise Pascal.

not feeling sorry for myself," Jewel says, "but I realized the world was a harsh place. I'd grown up with all my friends on welfare and I didn't want to struggle all my life. I felt helpless and I wanted a purpose. But what do you do? Become an environmental lawyer? Join Greenpeace? Shave your head? March?"

The answer for Jewel came one year later, when at 15 years of age she was asked to perform solo for the first time. Tom Bodet, an Alaskan radio personality, asked her to come on his *End of the Road Show* and sing. Jewel asked Nedra to help her prepare. Together, the two women rehearsed "Somewhere over the Rainbow," the hit song

Jewel practices the guitar on the campus of Interlochen, 1991. She taught herself to play the instrument while at the academy, a considerable achievement given that she struggled with dyslexia.

from *The Wizard of Oz*. Like the young Judy Garland, who had made the tune famous, Jewel was able to take the song and make it hers. It was during this performance that Jewel claims to have found her gift to the world—singing.

Of course, Jewel didn't spend all of her teenage years recording songs and sitting in a dimly lit library contemplating immortality. She was, for the most part, a fairly normal teen. The move from the farm to Anchorage meant being exposed to the popular music and fashion of the times, and at one point Jewel and some friends even formed a rap group called La Crème to perform in school talent shows. She also continued to perform with her father, who had added a woman named Suzanne Little to their act to form a trio called New Directions. Jewel's love of performing would soon lead her to a radical, and rewarding, change of scenery.

During the summer before her junior year of high

school Jewel was again wondering about the world outside of Alaska. Like most 16-year-olds, Jewel was looking ahead to her life as a young adult. Where would she live? What would she do for a living? So it was a stroke of luck when a teacher from the Interlochen Fine Arts Academy, a prestigious private school in Michigan, heard Jewel sing at a summer festival near Anchorage. The teacher persuaded Jewel to apply to Interlochen, where she could receive formal training in voice. Jewel won a scholarship for the final two years of high school. For someone with Jewel's immense talents it was a magical opportunity.

There was only one problem. Although the scholarship paid for 70 percent of her tuition, Jewel's parents could not afford the rest. So with the help of Nedra and her aunt Mossy, Jewel organized and sang at her first solo concert for the citizens of Homer. The concert helped pay for her first year at Interlochen, and hard work at summer jobs helped fill in the rest.

Interlochen proved to be all that the teacher had promised Jewel it would be. The prestigious private school was much more formal and strict than the public schools of Alaska. And most of her classmates at Interlochen had had years of formal training, instead of having sung folk music in a bunch of smoky bars. Jewel's own image of what going to Interlochen meant had to undergo a severe change. "Classical [singing] was hard for me," she says. "I went [there] thinking I'd [received] a scholarship for blues. They asked me to sing an aria and I didn't know what one was." (An aria is an elaborate melody sung by one person, often in an opera.)

Yet she attacked the classics with the same determination she'd shown when teaching herself to yodel at the age of six. Plunging headfirst into the study of opera, Jewel learned to use her voice and body as an instrument. She learned proper breathing techniques and how to control her wonderful falsetto, lessons that would be of great benefit to her as a pop music performer. And the difficult, strict academic policy helped Jewel develop self-discipline. Studying math, history, and science was all a part of attending the academy. But Jewel was also able to work on her writing while pursuing other artistic endeavors, such as painting, sculpture, and dance.

Focusing on music in such an intellectual manner did not sit well with Jewel though. She had been brought up in the folk tradition, where technique took a backseat to heart and emotion. For Jewel, opera lacked the immediate connection with the audience and was simply too rigid—there was no room for improvisation in opera. In fact, Jewel's unconventional upbringing once again caused her to stand out from her peers. While other students concentrated on a career in art, music, or dance, Jewel sang in piano bars in town to make money. She also posed for art classes and taught herself to play the guitar.

Along with making the long and painful discovery of the intricacies of playing guitar, she entered an extremely fertile period of songwriting at this time. Most of these early songs were influenced by her observations of the people around her interacting with one another and their environment. "I find people fascinating. . . ." she says. "I love every [messed-up] and beautiful thing about us." And she didn't just write the songs, she actually got a four-track tape recorder and made an 11-song demo tape, which unfortunately never reached the ears of any record producer. It's a testament to her homegrown talent that some of these early songs still show up in her live performances.

As usual, Jewel's restless spirit was not satisfied with just dancing, painting, singing, sculpting, and writing. She wanted to add to her repertoire of skills by taking up acting. However, at Interlochen, voice majors were not allowed to participate in the drama program. Perhaps for most voice majors this policy made sense. Even though operas are performed on a stage in front of an audience, the dramatic element is minor compared to the performer's ability to sing the difficult parts. In opera, emotion is presented mainly through the voice; facial expressions and body positions don't carry as much weight as they do in musical comedy, for instance. But there was no stopping the girl from Anchorage. With typical resolve, Jewel forced the school to allow her to audition for a part in the drama department's production of *Spoon River Anthology.* Not only did she get a part, she got the leading role, and the school changed its policy to allow students in majors other than theater to audition for plays in the drama program.

It was a wonderful, magical time for the talented young woman. Surrounded by others who, like her, were budding singers, writers, painters, and actors, Jewel lived mostly for the moment, not worrying about the future. But the future arrived anyway. In the summer of 1992 Jewel graduated from Interlochen. Like most recent high school graduates, she faced many options. She could try to get into a good college, she could move to New York and try to get work on Broadway, or she could look for a job and try to start a career. And like a lot of recent high school graduates, Jewel didn't know what to do. Michigan was a nice state to go to school in, but her family wasn't there. She missed the connection she had always felt with her parents and other relatives. After her experiences at Interlochen, though, Jewel knew that returning to Atz and the family farm would never suit her. She decided to join her mother, Nedra, who had moved to San Diego while Jewel was away at school.

Leaving the security and comfort of a familiar place and trying to create a new life somewhere strange is no easy task. Jewel had already done this several times in her 18 years: first, when her parents divorced; then when she went to live with her aunt in Hawaii for a few brief months in junior high; next, when she moved to Anchorage to be with her mom; and again when she moved to Michigan to attend Interlochen. Each time she had to leave friends and family along with familiar sights and places. And each time she conquered her fears and became stronger. But the move to San Diego was the most disruptive of her life.

No longer in school, no longer a child, Jewel was forced into the working world of adulthood. And it was nothing like Interlochen. With only a high school diploma, Jewel found her options limited. Jobs that had helped her pay for school—waitressing and cashier duties—didn't pay enough to support her and her mother, who also worked low-paying jobs. Though for a time she seemed to accept this situation, even the usually extremely positive Jewel became nervous about the future. "There was a time when I . . . had this realization that I didn't want to give up, and I would figure [things] out." Unfortunately Jewel's education didn't help her employment prospects. Her ability to sing arias or write poems didn't impress restaurant managers. They needed workers who were efficient and could get orders right. Customers wanted service, not singing.

Even when she found work, Jewel's desire to talk to people—to find out about their hopes and dreams, to share the lessons she had learned in her short life—didn't make her a popular employee, especially in restaurants. Jewel would spend so much time talking to customers that she would sometimes forget to take their orders. She couldn't help it; she was just naturally curious about what people wanted from life. "I believe people are basically good," she says. "We all come from the same place, we all have fear. We want to be loved. We all want passion in our lives. It doesn't matter if you're rich or homeless, it's all the same." Her natural empathy and interest in people's lives wasn't really a bad thing—many would agree that more people should be as friendly as Jewel. But it wasn't welcome on the job. She drifted from restaurant to restaurant barely making ends meet and wondering if things would ever get any better. "I wouldn't say I was suicidal," she says about this time in her life, "but I became consciously aware that I could not face time anymore. I think a lot of kids get to that place. You think, 'What . . . is the point? To have a family? Maybe, maybe not. To be a secretary?

A street scene from the Pacific Beach section of San Diego. After giving up her apartment, Jewel decided to park her van in this laid-back, somewhat bohemian neighborhood by the ocean—a decision that brought her into contact with other aspiring singers and musicians.

Maybe not. To be famous? Probably not.'"

Adding to her frustration may have been a chronic kidney problem, which created quite a trying experience in 1993. One day she awoke with a searing pain in her lower back. Nedra took Jewel to the nearest emergency room, only to be turned away because of a lack of medical insurance. Two hospitals and four clinics later, Jewel's kidney infection was finally treated. Though she recovered, Jewel had hit a physical and spiritual low point.

Seeing her daughter become more and more discouraged, Nedra knew something had to change if the talented young woman was to realize her dream. But first Jewel had to acknowledge the dream. With the insight that only a mother can have, Nedra saw that Jewel was destined for greatness. She knew that Jewel had a gift and that nothing should stop her from sharing that gift with the world. Nedra had watched Jewel grow up; she remembered the determination of the six-year-old learning to yodel. Facing the unknown with a sense of adventure had led Jewel to school in Michigan, thousands of miles from her family and friends. Nedra knew that with her support and love Jewel could face anything and succeed.

To make sure she was on the right track, Nedra questioned Jewel about her long-term plans, her dreams, what she wanted to do with her life. "I want to sing to remind people to live their dreams," the girl replied. Confident that Jewel could succeed if given a chance, Nedra then made a radical suggestion: the two women would move out of their apartment and live in a couple of vans. Without having to pay rent and utilities and all the other costs of an apartment, they would be able to work low-paying jobs and still have time for Jewel to write songs and perform. As might be expected, Jewel didn't immediately agree with this plan.

Who could blame her? To willingly become homeless is not a decision to be made lightly. Saving money and having time to work on her music were only one side of the equation. Living in a van, washing her hair at a local discount store, and enduring the humiliation of being homeless were among the negatives. Plus there was no guarantee that she would achieve her dream. "A lot of us just aren't taught that something you love can make you money," Jewel says. "It wasn't until I got fired from my last job that I decided, that's it. I don't care. I'd rather die and drop out of the world than wake up every day and be so unhappy."

Although Jewel was adventurous and brave, she still had misgivings. She asked, "Maybe I should have a fall-back plan?" But Nedra remained firm. "If you have a fall-back plan, you will fall back," she told Jewel. "You are young. Be brave. Have faith in yourself."

Used to a life of meager means in Alaska, Jewel had little problem adjusting to life in her van. She wore secondhand clothes and ate mainly peanut butter and carrots. Of course, it wasn't easy. She had to endure cruel stares and cutting comments from people in the local Kmart and Denny's, where she used the restroom to wash her hair.

But there were happy times as well. Without the pressure of keeping an apartment or a job she hated, Jewel was able to spend all her time on her writing. Most of the songs that would eventually make up her first album were written during this time. Laced with a biting reality, the lyrics are also full of hope and encouragement. "It's so easy to feel alone and to feel like you're the only one going through whatever you're going through," Jewel says. "Especially when you're young, when you're around 18. When I was that age, I was so thankful for what little pieces of encouragement I got. I know that my music does that."

Another thing Jewel was thankful for was having chosen San Diego as her home base. Of course, part of the reason had been that her mother was living there. But in the long run San Diego also proved to be the perfect place for a talent like Jewel. Although Los Angeles will always be the center of the entertainment universe, in the early 1990s attention was focused on Seattle as the source of exciting new music. But down in San Diego, Jewel was able to be part of a mellow scene where the artists were more concerned with creating good, meaningful music than with hitching their wagons onto the latest hot thing. Low-key San Diego acts such as Mojo Nixon and the Beat Farmers were creating a small but influential stir in the music business.

More specifically, Jewel was attracted to the small coastal community of Pacific Beach, just south of San Diego's metropolis. Removed from the tract housing and strip malls of suburbia, Pacific Beach was a bohemian community of surfers, artists, writers, and singers. It was a place where Jewel finally felt she belonged. "We were all

The Beatles (from left: George Harrison, John Lennon, Ringo Starr, Paul McCartney) may have been pop music's most influential group ever. Because of her unusual upbringing, however, Jewel heard very little of their work until after she had graduated from high school.

starving," she says, "but here are all these talented, brilliant writers—I just felt so honored to be around them and writing with them."

The focus of all this creative energy was a coffeehouse called the Innerchange. At first Jewel was simply a loyal patron who hung out at the Innerchange to enjoy some coffee and delight in the creativity flowing around her. Here she met a kindred spirit in local folksinger Steve Poltz, who was part of a band called the Rugburns. Poltz, an old hand at writing and singing songs, helped Jewel refine her poetry into a more common verse-chorus-verse style that audiences were familiar with. He also helped her take herself less seriously, showing her how to inject a bit of humor into her performances. Most important, he introduced her to pop culture, especially the music that she should know: the Beatles, Neil Young, Paul Simon. As Jewel remembers, "[Steve Poltz] used to take me to his house and say, 'This is "Let it Be."' He laid it all out for me because I wasn't raised listening to music." The two soon became close friends.

Although Jewel's spiral notebooks were filled with poems, observations, and the beginnings of songs, she hadn't yet had a chance to present herself to the world as Jewel, the folksinger. One problem was the difficulty she had learning to play the guitar. She'd been playing for a little more than a year, but her dyslexia made it difficult for her to learn at anything more than a walking pace. She even claimed that she had to practice 20 times harder than other people just to learn the basic chords. But she was determined to add guitar playing to her repertoire, just as she had been determined to yodel.

More of a writer than a musician, despite her classical training, Jewel had to discover for herself the secrets of chord changes and melodies. But with the help of Poltz and other local musicians, Jewel eventually felt confident enough to audition for a regular stint at the Innerchange. Her beautiful voice, earnest songwriting, and youthful exuberance quickly convinced Nancy Porter, owner of the Innerchange, to give her a spot every Thursday night. "She was really rough, [but] she had the talent," says Porter. "She disciplined herself and kept at it. I knew she'd succeed."

Success wasn't going to be easy, though. In 1993, there weren't very many people who wanted to hear a 19-year-old folksinger, much less one who put childhood poems to music and had been playing guitar for only a year. Talented or not, Jewel had her work cut out for her.

On the day of her first Innerchange gig Jewel stood on street corners all over Pacific Beach handing out fliers announcing her show. Innocent as she was, the response—

San Diego–based folksinger Steve Poltz helped Jewel refine her songwriting and improve her stage presence. Poltz also cowrote two songs that would appear on Jewel's debut album, including the hit "You Were Meant for Me."

or lack thereof—disappointed her somewhat. Not too many people seemed interested, and Jewel went back to her van that afternoon with a sense of impending doom. When she got to the Innerchange that evening for the show, she was almost sick to her stomach. There were plenty of empty seats, and it looked as if the majority of her audience would be employees of the Innerchange rather than paying customers.

It wasn't easy, but Jewel overcame her disappointment enough to go onstage and do her show. She may have been an inexperienced solo artist, but she wasn't an inexperienced performer. Drawing on her years of singing in Alaskan bars, as well as the lessons she'd learned from seasoned performers such as her father and Steve Poltz, Jewel steeled herself against embarrassment and disappointment. She went through her entire set as if playing to a packed house rather than six paying patrons.

In one very important way playing to a less-than-full house was good for Jewel. The weeks, which turned into months, of playing to sparse audiences gave her a chance to work the bugs out of her material as well as develop her patter—the jokes and stories that filled the time between songs. She also began a tradition that would continue even after she became famous. During the show Jewel would stop periodically to genuinely thank the audience for coming, expressing her gratitude with her usual honesty and heart. After all, Jewel was finally living her dream, even if she had taken home only five dollars that first night.

This honesty and freshness was Jewel's real personality shining through, not some phony act. "I remember the first time I saw her perform," said Jewel's first manager, Inga Vainshtein. "She reminded me of Barbra Streisand meets Meryl Streep." Remembering the days when she sang with her father in the bars of Alaska, Jewel knew that the reason people came to see her was to be entertained, not instructed. In fact, Jewel never really considered herself a singer-songwriter, an artist, or a performer. "I'm an entertainer," she says. "It's a craft, and I like that." Jewel knew that her audience was responsible for her being onstage. Without them she was simply a surfer girl writing poems on the beach.

Jewel's relationship with Nancy Porter and the Innerchange was one of mutual satisfaction and support. Porter needed someone to draw coffee-drinking crowds into her club, and Jewel needed an audience. "[The Innerchange] was looking for business. They said I could keep the door money, and they would keep the coffee sales," Jewel says. "And so I stuck with them and we both struggled together to get more people to come in."

Even though it may not have been the perfect venue for a musician, Jewel didn't mind at all. Having played in rough roadhouses in Alaska, Jewel found the slightly noisy, yet intimate and clean, atmosphere of the Innerchange a welcome relief. After every performance, many of which lasted more than three hours, Jewel would stand at the exit to thank her growing number of fans personally as they left.

Such innocence and genuine charm goes a long way, but no one would keep coming back to see the same performer time and again if the music wasn't any good. But the music *was* good, and a refreshing change from the classic-rock cover bands (groups that perform songs originally performed by other bands or singers) that frequently play small clubs.

The combination of her beautiful voice and inspiring music began to draw larger and larger crowds. Of course, Jewel's physical beauty didn't go unnoticed. Lou Niles, a DJ at a local modern-rock radio station, had befriended the lovely surfer girl soon after she arrived in San Diego. He knows she has talent, but he thinks her looks also had a lot to do with her early success. "If she were three hundred pounds and missing an arm, people wouldn't have checked her out so much," says Niles.

Jewel isn't exactly flattered by such remarks. "I think the images and standards we have of beauty are unrealistic," she says. "I think the idea that a woman feels flattered when she's complimented on her beauty is archaic."

Whatever the reason, her audience kept coming back, and Jewel's regular Thursday night gig soon became the biggest night at the Innerchange. Jewel had become such a huge draw that even raising ticket prices from three to five dollars didn't stop the crowds from coming in.

Jewel's songs, most of them written after she moved into her van, really connected with the audience. "Who Will Save Your Soul"—the song that would eventually make Jewel a household name—suggests that life is less than perfect but is also an optimistic refusal to let a less-than-perfect world bring Jewel down. This, combined with her youthful beauty and otherworldly voice, kept them coming back for more.

The dynamic combination also got her noticed by recording companies, which had been waiting for the next big thing to follow the success of "grunge" rock coming out of the Seattle music scene. By late fall of 1993 word had spread to Los Angeles, home of the biggest record companies in the world, that an unusual and unsigned talent had surfaced in San Diego. Buzz from local media and a cut of the song "Who Will Save Your Soul" on a CD of local music put out by the cutting-edge rock station 91X helped fuel the fire. From as far away as New York, record company A&R (artists and repertoire) executives began migrating to Pacific Beach on Thursday nights to check out the rising star known as Jewel.

Signing a new artist is a career-risking gamble for A&R execs. Perhaps they hear of a new group or singer through the grapevine. They check out this new artist at various live performances. They take the artist out to dinner to get to know the personal side of the individual (or group) they are considering signing. They listen to demo tapes. Then, based on all this information and the executive's own experience, the decision may be made to recommend that the record company offer the artist a contract. The problem is, the listening public may or may not like the artist as much as the record company people do. Then again, the record company may have just signed the next Beatles or Backstreet Boys. Will the artist be a one-hit wonder? Will he or she be able to sustain popularity—or ever achieve any in the first place? Can the record company make back all the millions it spent to win the artist over, do demo tapes, make

David Grohl (left), Kurt Cobain (center), and Krist Novoselic stormed onto the music scene as the band Nirvana. The same Atlantic Record executives who were responsible for unleashing the "grunge" phenomenon eventually signed Jewel.

the first record, promote it, and send the act out on tour? A smart pick can send an agent straight to the top, with fancy cars, a big house, and job promotions. A bad pick, however, can mean a one-way ticket out of the business.

Because the stakes are so high, some agents tend to appeal to an artist's greed and vanity rather than to things like career goals. Luckily for Jewel, she attracted the attention of Inga Vainshtein, a former movie executive who knew a talent executive from Atlantic Records named Jenny Price. So on a Thursday night in 1994, the two women drove down from L.A. to the Innerchange to watch Jewel perform. Price was impressed not just by Jewel's craft and voice, but by the effect she had on the crowd. "What I noticed was how completely silent the crowd was when Jewel sang," says Price. Rushing back to Los Angeles that night, Price could hardly wait to call her boss and tell him of her discovery.

Her boss was Danny Goldberg, president of Atlantic Records and the man responsible for unleashing grunge band sensation Nirvana on what had been the stale pop-music scene. Price knew she had something exciting with Jewel, but convincing Goldberg of it would take all of her patience and skill—and Jewel's cooperation. Price was well respected in her industry and had an ear for talent, but she was still young at only 28 years of age. To convince the man who had discovered Nirvana that the next big thing was a young homeless woman singing folk songs she'd written while living in a van by the ocean would not be an easy task. But Goldberg was the sort of executive who knew when to trust his employees. If Price was willing to take a risk on Jewel, he thought, perhaps it was worth looking into. He told Price to have Jewel come to Los Angeles with her guitar to play for him in his office. It was the break Price—and Jewel—had been hoping for.

Jewel first made a name for herself performing in small venues throughout the United States. The intimate atmosphere allowed her to connect with her audience, helping to create a loyal fan base.

4

TURNING POINT

CONVINCING DANNY GOLDBERG to hear Jewel play was a big first step. But getting a contract for her with Atlantic Records was still not going to be easy. A few days after Goldberg agreed to listen to Jewel, Jenny Price set up a meeting in L.A. Price hoped that once Goldberg actually saw Jewel perform, rather than just hearing her, he would realize there was more to her act than a heavenly voice. Unfortunately, a rather large problem developed.

As Goldberg, Price, and a few other record company honchos waited patiently, Jewel and Nedra were busy taking one wrong turn after another. Perhaps it was stress, or simply L.A.'s confusing highway system, but whatever the reason, the two San Diegans were soon hopelessly lost. After waiting nearly an hour without sight or sound of Jewel, Danny Goldberg was forced to leave so he could attend to other business. Price tried hard to get him to stay a bit longer and give Jewel a chance, but he was a busy man and couldn't afford to miss meetings waiting for a teenage folksinger to show up. So he left, and Price's dream of signing Jewel with Atlantic began to fade away.

Two hours after Goldberg's departure, Jewel and Nedra arrived at the Atlantic Records office. Frustrated, embarrassed, and feeling out of her element, Jewel nonetheless played for Price and the other Atlantic employees still waiting to hear her. Once again, the years of playing in roadhouses and in front of small yet highly critical audiences paid off for Jewel. Price was again impressed not only with the music but with Jewel's stage presence—including the fact that this young girl could seem so confident and at ease in such a high-pressure setting. That would be an important trait for Jewel to have if she was going to survive the meat grinder of fame that pop music stars must go through.

But as impressed as she and the other executives were, Price knew it didn't mean anything without Goldberg's approval. So she offered Jewel a chance to make a demo tape at Atlantic's expense, with no strings attached. Jewel took the offer, went to a recording studio in Hollywood, and laid down around 30 songs for just one man—one very important man—to listen to.

Unfortunately, Goldberg remained noncommittal even after hearing the demo. Price could have given up at this point; in fact, most A&R people would have. But she saw something more in Jewel than just the next pop star. For Price, Jewel was not a fad, like grunge or punk rock or disco. Jewel was a sincere, caring human being with an extraordinary gift. Price believed it would be a shame if Atlantic couldn't help Jewel share that gift with the world. So she kept at Goldberg, never letting him forget about the blond singer-songwriter in San Diego. Finally she convinced him to make the journey down to the Innerchange to check out Jewel's regular Thursday night gig.

The day after Goldberg finally saw Jewel perform in San Diego, all of Price's faith and determination paid off. Goldberg called her into his office and gave her the green light to sign Jewel to a contract. But he didn't think Jewel was just good—he thought she was great. He told Price,

"You were absolutely right. She's a career artist."

Jenny Price was ecstatic. Her instinct about Jewel and her persistence had paid off. The next big step, though, was to get Jewel to sign with Atlantic Records. Jewel may have been young and fairly inexperienced, but she wasn't stupid. Living in a van tends to make a person a bit suspicious of things that seem too good to be true. Jewel also had her mother on her side. Nedra was definitely not young or innocent; in fact, she presented quite an unnerving persona to the record company agents who had begun to flock to Jewel's Thursday night gigs.

Along with Nedra, though, Jewel also had the experience and connections of Inga Vainshtein on her side. Vainshtein joined Nedra in managing Jewel's career. It was Vainshtein who had first suggested to Jenny Price that Jewel was worth looking at, and it was she who now pushed Jewel and Nedra toward signing with Atlantic. For Jewel the decision wasn't a tough one. She had liked Jenny Price's approach to business from the very start, had appreciated the chance to cut the no-strings-attached demo, and, once she met him, had liked the way Danny Goldberg treated his artists. In the end Jewel signed a multi-album deal with Atlantic. Suddenly she had a new apartment for herself and Nedra, a used Volvo station wagon, and a brand-spanking-new guitar.

Jewel was also suddenly expected to handle herself as a professional artist. In a typical situation the transition from teenager to working professional can be pretty intimidating. So it seems reasonable to assume that Jewel felt a bit nervous after signing her recording contract with Atlantic. One day she was a carefree folksinger living in a van near her favorite beach in San Diego, and the next she was a "career artist" signed with one of the biggest recording companies in the world. She was expected to record an album that would make tons of money. She was expected to put aside exhaustion and a good portion of her privacy in order to promote the new album.

More important, she would have to put aside the creative aspect of writing songs for the more businesslike approach of recording an album. There was studio time to book, a producer to hire, backup musicians to audition, and many more intricate details that she would need to attend to as part of making an album. She'd have to hit the road on her own, appear on talk shows, and grant newspaper interviews to support the album. There were legions of assistants to help out with most of these tasks, but it would be Jewel's name on the album cover and her songs burned onto the small plastic discs. As she had so many times before, the young woman from Homer, Alaska, shouldered the responsibility and eagerly embraced the future.

First, Jewel had to go through the nearly four hours of material that made up her live show and choose the songs that would work best on an album. What sounded good at a cozy coffeehouse might not work too well in a studio. Luckily Jewel's friend Steve Poltz, who had some experience with studio recording, helped her with this task. Meanwhile, Atlantic searched for a producer, a studio, backup musicians, and all the other people it takes to make a record. Producer Ben Keith, who had worked with other famous singer-songwriters, including Neil Young and James Taylor, was hired. Jewel said, "I was looking for a producer who wouldn't produce me. . . . I was looking for somebody who would at least let me be who I was, so I could be honest and recognizable to myself and my fans. I went with Ben Keith for those reasons."

Jewel's decision to sign with Atlantic had been based partly on the personal relationship she had built with Jenny Price and Danny Goldberg. Because they believed in Jewel's long-term potential, they weren't concerned so much with whipping out a multiplatinum album. Instead, they had a real interest in developing Jewel as an artist and allowing her to mature at her own pace. Price and Goldberg also knew from personal experience that a large part of Jewel's appeal was her live act. To capture that for an

Rock star Neil Young in concert. Jewel recorded the bulk of her debut album, Pieces of You, *at Young's studio, and she lists the Canadian-born singer-songwriter as one of her musical idols.*

album, they arranged for a crew, along with the necessary equipment, to head down to the Innerchange for two nights to record Jewel in front of her home crowd.

For the regulars at the Innerchange, seeing one of the four, three-hour sets on July 28 and 29, 1994, wasn't easy. Not only had the cover charge been jacked up to eight dollars, but unless you showed up early or were supremely lucky, you didn't have a chance of getting in. Those who did manage to get a ticket may look back years from now and realize that they witnessed a golden moment in pop music history: Jewel's transformation from beach-bunny folkie to big-time recording artist.

Initially, most radio stations ignored Pieces of You, *while music critics dismissed Jewel's songs as little more than the musings of an adolescent.*

But Atlantic wasn't about to leave the future of its new career artist in the hands of a live crowd. The balance of the album would be recorded in Neil Young's Redwood Digital Studio in Woodside, California, with some members of Young's studio band, the Stray Gators, hired to help out. Jewel also got help from Charlotte Caffey, the guitar player for the 1980s all-girl pop group the Go-Go's. Of course Steve Poltz would also be there for his friend.

In February 1995 Jewel's debut album, *Pieces of You*, was released. Jewel celebrated by performing at two sold-out shows in San Diego's Hahn Cosmopolitan Theatre. It was at once a joyful celebration of a new life and a tearful good-bye to the city and people who had nurtured the budding artist. At the end of the second show Jewel gave a short thank-you to the town that had supported her, including these words:

> My fellow music lovers . . . I was just a girl who was tired of waitressing, and people believed in me and fed me by coming to my shows. . . . Sometimes record labels think they sell albums—but they don't—they help, but it's you guys who help me. So often our dreams become our hobbies and it deadens our passions. I love my life and want to thank you all. I know our lives are separate and that none of you have to care about my happiness, but that you do things like taking the time to call radio stations means a lot to me.

This joyous time in Jewel's life would be overshadowed in the following months as *Pieces of You* got off to a slow start, falling short even of Atlantic's conservative sales estimates. The first single, "Who Will Save Your Soul," was getting limited airplay on most radio stations, if it got any at all. It began to seem that all the hard work and sacrifice had been for nothing. Lots of talented young people try to make it in show business each year, but only a tiny fraction of them ever go on to stardom. Jewel began to worry about which side of the statistics she would fall on.

Jewel's wholesome image and refreshing optimism appealed to fans. Her "coffeehouse tour" was an innovative way to take her folksy style on the road.

5

BREAKING THROUGH

IN 1995 THE GRUNGE ROCK OF NIRVANA and the gangsta rap of Snoop Doggy Dogg and Dr. Dre dominated the radio airwaves. The music was hard edged, cynical, angry, and laced with references to cheap sex, drugs, and alcohol. But it improved ratings and sold records, and that was what mattered most to radio station managers and record company executives. Jewel's debut album was seen by many as a much-needed antidote to this mix of aggressive, violent music. Her songs were positive and spoke of the human ability to change the world through love and peace. Jewel wanted people to work together to make the earth a better place. The problem was, no one seemed to want to hear that.

Despite her ability to attract sellout crowds at the Innerchange, Jewel was finding it difficult to get noticed amid an abundance of young "alternative" musicians. *Pieces of You* was selling fewer than 500 copies a week, and except for some brief airtime on easy-listening stations, the single "Who Will Save Your Soul" went unnoticed. Music critics for major newspapers and lifestyle magazines lavished praise on the hard-edged rock and rap acts that were deemed hip. The critics really didn't know what to make of Jewel, so they made fun of her innocence and beautiful voice and refused to admit that she might be a serious artist.

Her youthfulness—she was only 21—also worked against her. Many musicians spend 10 years or more establishing themselves and their talent. Yet here was Jewel, barely out of high school, with a record contract. It just wasn't supposed to happen that way. Of the cool reception *Pieces of You* initially got, Jewel would later remark, "The climate was different. It was the height of grunge and cynicism, and everything I was saying was trying to counter cynicism. It took the climate to change before the record could do well."

Of course, changing the musical taste of every record buyer was a formidable—even an impossible—task. But Jewel couldn't just sit around and do nothing as her record faltered. Having put so much of her time and energy into becoming a recording artist, Jewel was not about to give up just because some people didn't like her record. In fact, Jewel later said that it wasn't important for her to have a multiplatinum album. "In the beginning, a lot of radio stations said [my music] was unplayable, and video shows and TV stations said it was unlistenable. Which was fine, because I never expected to sell a lot of albums with this one. It was just supposed to be a time capsule of where I was."

Atlantic's promotional machine decided that the best way to bring Jewel to the attention of the public was to try to re-create her success at the Innerchange at similar venues across the country. Enlisting the aid of Nedra and Inga Vainshtein, the strongest pillars in Jewel's support system, the record label began booking the young singer at coffeehouses and smaller clubs throughout the United States and Canada. The plan was to put her in a rotation at various clubs in four different cities for four weeks at a time. This meant that when she wasn't playing a gig, she was driving to the next one. It was Jewel, a road manager, and a Ford van, traveling the highways and byways of America. Rather than becoming discouraged by this grueling schedule, however, Jewel remained realistic yet optimistic. Looking back on this time, she remembers knowing that the hard work would pay off. "I never expected to sell a lot of albums," she says. "If I wanted to have a long-term career like Neil Young, it would just take touring."

The venues Jewel had to play on the road were far different from the comfortable, low-key setting of the Innerchange. For one thing, there was no local audience filled with friends and well-wishers eager to hear her sing and tell funny stories for more than three hours. The first big change Atlantic asked Jewel to make was to limit her performances to less than two hours. This was to save her voice and also to get her to the next gig on time. Then there was the hard task of breaking in a new audience.

The first gig in a new venue was always difficult for Jewel. Generally, few people showed up, and she was in a strange town far from home. Yet by the third or fourth show, the crowd would be larger and more friendly. Atlantic's Jenny Price had figured it would go this way. She says, "[Jewel is] just so incredibly talented that we knew as soon as she got in front of people she could win them over." And so, time and time again, Jewel—young, eager, and talented—would take the stage in some college town, play for a sparse crowd for a few nights, and move on. Then, time and again, she would return a few weeks later to a larger, more welcoming crowd. They say Rome wasn't built in a day, and neither was Jewel's success.

In addition to replicating the cozy atmosphere of the Innerchange to bring out the best in Jewel, Atlantic's promotional machine wanted to make sure she was reaching an audience that could empathize and grow with her—namely, women of high school and college age. Not only did the plan include keeping her away from more traditional college bar venues, it also meant playing at high school auditoriums.

Although Jewel wanted to reach young kids with her message of hope, playing before crowds of unruly students wasn't the way she had planned it. On one occasion Jewel was booked to play at an inner-city high school in Detroit. As she waited backstage to go on, Jewel was happy to hear how excited the kids were for her to come out. They were singing her name and seemed much more into it than most high school audiences had been. But once she hit the stage, she was in for a shock. The kids had been expecting a rapper with the same name, and their disappointment at a young girl with a guitar singing folk songs was palpable. In fact, most of the students actually got up and walked out.

In time, Jewel would move away from the coffeehouses and high schools. Although Atlantic wanted her to get as much exposure as possible, the record company seemed to have a problem finding appropriate touring mates for her. For a brief stretch she was the opening act for Peter Murphy, the former lead singer for the British Goth band Bauhaus. Each night for six weeks Jewel went before crowds of black-robed, pale-faced Goths with their teeth filed into fangs. A few months later she was booked at a summer music festival in Washington, D.C., with rock bands such as the Foo Fighters, Everclear, and the Afghan Whigs. As she launched into the second song of her set, Jewel was hit in the head by a Frisbee thrown by someone in the audience. This time, though, her pride overcame her work ethic. She stopped playing, thanked the crowd, and walked off the stage.

The trials of touring wore at Jewel's spirit. But she continued to plug along, going where the record label told her to go, playing before mostly unappreciative—or worse, completely apathetic—crowds. What kept her going through all this was the lesson she had learned so many years ago while singing with her dad in Alaskan bars and roadhouses: People came to shows to have their spirits raised. At the time, she told a reporter, "I'm not doing this

Peter Murphy, former lead singer for the British Goth band Bauhaus. Jewel opened for Murphy, and for other artists with whom she had nothing in common, because Atlantic Records was trying to get her as much exposure as possible.

for fame or money. I'm doing it because it serves my spirit and it reminds people to live their dreams. That's needed in the world now." So Jewel continued touring from city to city, never complaining or letting down her small but increasing fan base.

Despite her dedication, Jewel was finding it difficult to get a break with music critics and radio stations. So Atlantic began promoting Jewel as a young female artist (instead of, for example, promoting her in terms of her style of music). The idea was to try to take advantage of the growing popularity of female singer-songwriters in an industry that had been dominated by men since the days of Buddy Holly and Elvis Presley. Instead of getting a boost,

Initially Juliana Hatfield (at right) and the other "Atlantic women" may have overshadowed Jewel. But before too long Everyday Angels, as Jewel's fans called themselves, created a groundswell of support for her music, phoning radio stations to request Jewel's songs and buying her albums.

however, Jewel seemed to get lost in the shuffle. The problem was that Jewel wasn't the only female singer-songwriter signed to Atlantic. The "Atlantic women," as they were called, included such artists as Jill Sobule, Melissa Ferrick, Juliana Hatfield, and Victoria Williams. Unlike Jewel, most of these women were already established artists who, although their albums hadn't gone platinum by any means, were either media darlings or at least cult favorites.

The music critics loved Williams's southern sensibility, Sobule's quirkiness, and Hatfield's punk origins as the former singer with the Blake Babies. They got the attention, and Jewel was ignored. To make matters worse, Danny Goldberg, the man who had given the green light to Jewel's signing with Atlantic, left the company in late 1994. If it weren't for the support of Jenny Price and the hard work of Nedra and Inga Vainshtein, it's probable that Jewel would have either given up or been released from her contract. As it was, she kept touring, writing—and hoping.

Even though radio stations still wouldn't play her songs, and the critics continued to make fun of her music, her innocence, and even her crooked teeth, the people who mattered most to Jewel began to respond. With every live performance Jewel's fan base grew, and as the fan base grew, so did the requests to radio stations for her songs. Responding not just to the music but also to Jewel's message, her fans began calling themselves Everyday Angels, after a line in her song "I'm Sensitive." One of the biggest breaks for Jewel came when she was given the chance to open for Liz Phair, a controversial yet popular female artist. And after Jewel played nearly 500 shows in a year, her single "Who Will Save Your Soul" began getting airtime in some of the larger radio markets, such as Los Angeles, Houston, and New York. At the same time, sales of *Pieces of You* picked up enough for Atlantic to mount a bigger promotional campaign.

Just when Jewel had decided to come off the road for a while to write songs for a second album, Atlantic decided to put her back out there—this time with a full touring entourage—to pump up sales even more. But that's how show business works sometimes, and Jewel was learning a lot about self-promotion and hard work. "You can ride the horse, or it can ride you," she says about the music business. "I'm going to ride the horse as best as I can." The company rereleased the single "Who Will Save Your Soul," which peaked at number 11 on the *Billboard* magazine singles chart of the most popular songs in September 1996. Jewel's second single "You Were Meant for Me," cowritten with Steve Poltz, made it to the number two spot by November of the same year. Jewel's video for "You Were Meant for Me" won Best Female Video at the 1996 MTV Video Music Awards, an accolade that depended on the votes of music fans rather than the opinions of music critics.

Even though it had taken more than a year for *Pieces of You* to get even minimal airplay, Jewel now found herself an "overnight" success. Suddenly she was everywhere: in TV interviews; on the covers of such magazines as *Time, Rolling Stone,* and *Interview;* on the radio and the music-video stations MTV and VH1. After seeing the up-and-coming star on a late-night talk show, the actor Sean Penn declared her "the female Bob Dylan" and commissioned her to write a song for his movie *The Crossing Guard.* He also took a shot at directing the video for "You Were Meant for Me." Then at the 1995 Venice Film Festival the paparazzi—photographers who sometimes go to extreme measures to photograph celebrities—went nuts for Sean Penn and his new girlfriend, Jewel.

This was Jewel's first taste of what it meant to be a celebrity. Her brief romance with Penn was front-page news on every tabloid in the United States for months. Although the relationship with Penn didn't last, the wisdom she gained from that experience on how to deal with celebrity would serve her well in the future. For someone so young, Jewel was surprisingly able to resist the temptations that sudden celebrity can bring. "The focus of my life was never glamour or fame," she says rather matter-of-factly, "so now [that] I am in the music business I don't feel overly caught up in it. I don't need it, and if I did, that would scare me."

Of course, show business has its good side as well as its bad. But, Jewel's success was a bit like Cinderella's life after the prince fits the glass slipper on her foot. "It's like a Datsun pickup winning the Indy 500," is how she puts it. Not only was she getting accolades in the form of inter-

Jewel, seen here at the 1996 MTV Video Music Awards, began to get a taste of life as a celebrity after Pieces of You *went platinum. Suddenly a regular on the music video stations, she also graced the covers of numerous magazines.*

views and awards, but she was also beginning to get offers from outside the pop music industry. The first sign that Jewel might be more than a simple folksinger came late in 1995. Because the song "Somewhere over the Rainbow" from *The Wizard of Oz* was a staple of her live show, the producers of a special benefit production of the movie for the Children's Defense Fund cast her in the role of Dorothy. Taped live at New York's Lincoln Center and

Jewel performs with Melissa Etheridge, an artist she had admired for years, on the VH1 show Duets. *Jewel was all over the small screen the night the episode debuted, appearing in TNT's* The Wizard of Oz *as well.*

broadcast on the cable station TNT, the show included such luminaries as Roger Daltrey, Jackson Browne, Nathan Lane, Natalie Cole, and Debra Winger.

Coincidentally, Jewel was seen that very same night on VH1, as she joined Melissa Etheridge on a previously recorded episode of the now defunct *Duets* program, one of the most popular shows on the video music channel at the time. More high-profile TV appearances were to follow throughout 1996. Jewel was a guest on the late-night talk shows of Conan O'Brien and Jay Leno, and she was interviewed on *Entertainment Tonight.* She was also finally able to break onto MTV with appearances on episodes of *Alternative Nation* and *120 Minutes,* which showcased young artists who received little exposure from typical radio and video shows because their music was considered "alternative" or different from the mainstream.

Sales of *Pieces of You,* which had begun to pick up because of Jewel's broadened appeal, were rapidly approaching a total of 200,000. Atlantic decided to take advantage of the increase in popularity and rerecord the live version of "Who Will Save Your Soul" from the Inner-change sessions to make it more radio friendly. It worked. The number one rock station in the country, KROQ in Los Angeles, put the single into rotation shortly after its release. For the formerly homeless surfer girl, life was indeed becoming a fairy tale. "I never thought it would be on this level," she said at the time. "I don't mean so much the level of success but . . . knowing that for the rest of my life, I'm going to be OK. That's so amazing."

A long way from the coffeehouse circuit: Jewel sings for a huge crowd on the final day of Woodstock '99. With millions of loyal fans and two hit albums under her belt, the woman from Homer had the pop music world in the palm of her hand. Never afraid to take a risk, though, she branched out into other artistic endeavors, including a book of poetry and a motion picture role.

6

BRANCHING OUT

JEWEL'S INITIAL SUCCESS didn't ruin her work ethic at all. From her childhood in Homer, Alaska, Jewel had developed the practice of writing every day. Even with her successes and her busy schedule, she continued to set aside time each day simply to write in her journal. Her thoughts, snippets of poetry, and ideas for new songs all went into a series of battered spiral notebooks. So when it came time for her to go into the studio to begin work on another album, she had plenty of material.

During the summer of 1996, in between taping shows for MTV, headlining her own tour, and posing for the cover of *Rolling Stone* magazine, Jewel went through the process of finding a producer, a backup band, and studio time. For the production of the new album Atlantic put her up in the Bearsville Studios in Woodstock, New York. Meanwhile, some of Jewel's most hard-core fans had established an online fan club called Everyday Angels. When some members of Everyday Angels in the Woodstock area found out that Jewel was nearby, they organized a massive appeal for a free, private concert. Jewel was more than happy to treat the fans who had been so instrumental in her success. Of course, the wide reach of the Internet ensured that Everyday Angels from all over the country soon learned of the event that was being called Jewelstock. Soon the intimate, private concert turned into a two-day affair complete with opening acts and a small donation to preserve the Bearsville Theatre, where it was held.

The second album, meanwhile, had to take a backseat to the first one, which was still selling like hotcakes. Atlantic was hesitant to release a new album that might compete with the first one, so the product was temporarily shelved. In the meantime, Jewel continued her grueling schedule on the road. Not only was she sometimes headlining her own tours, but the artists she now toured with were superstars such as Neil Young and Bob Dylan. Late in 1996 she made an appearance at the Tibetan Freedom Festival, organized by Adam Yauch, a member of the rap group the Beastie Boys, and she covered the Democratic National Convention as a reporter for MTV. Before the year was out she had also recorded songs for the soundtracks of the movies *I Shot Andy Warhol, Phenomenon,* and *The Craft.*

If 1996 was the year of Jewel's big breakthrough, 1997 was the year she began to prove her staying power. Following all the hoopla with magazine covers and MTV appearances, Jewel was offered a spot on Sarah McLachlan's highly touted Lilith Fair tour for the summer of '97. The idea behind the tour was to show off the strength and energy of women in pop music. Along with headliner McLachlan and Jewel, the tour featured artists such as Paula Cole and Sheryl Crow.

Since the days of playing at the Innerchange, Jewel had been either an opening act or a headliner. On the Lilith Fair circuit, however, she had flashbacks to when she used to play at the Alaskan roadhouses with her parents as part of a group. Although she still performed on her own at Lilith, the close-knit community of female pop stars made it seem more like a group than a collection of solo performers. In

Jewel threw her support behind the Tibetan Freedom Concert, organized by Adam Yauch to protest China's occupation of Tibet. Seen here at the Freedom Concert is Yauch's group, the Beastie Boys.

fact, at the end of each show all the women would get onstage together to sing Joni Mitchell's "Big Yellow Taxi" as an affirmation of their beliefs and sisterhood.

Once again, however, Jewel had to endure the cynicism of the press and the music establishment. Not only was it hard for McLachlan to get backing for her tour—most music industry executives thought the idea of an all-female music festival would fail—she also had to face the negative reviews once the festival was under way. Jewel had heard it all before. It was the same rock establishment that had told her in 1994 that no one wanted to listen to a woman playing an acoustic guitar and singing folk songs about being sensitive or saving the world. Only this time she had three singles on the charts, and her touring mates were no slouches either. Sheryl Crow, Paula Cole, and Meredith Brooks were all getting heavy rotation on MTV and radio, and although each had her own style, there was no denying the girl power on the stage every night. And for Jewel it was an affirmation of her own belief that "optimism is a choice. . . . Innocence isn't ever really lost; we just need to maintain it."

One way that Jewel maintains her own innocence is through her writing. Even as she maintained a grueling concert schedule, Jewel began to organize the poems she had been writing since she was 15. The resulting book was published in May of 1998 under the title *A Night Without Armor: Poems.* As part of her publishing deal Harper-Collins paid Jewel $2 million for the book of poems and a memoir, *Chasing Down the Dawn,* which was released in October 2000.

Although most critics panned the poetry book—and even Jewel admitted that it would never have been published without the benefit of her multiplatinum album—her music fans helped it become the first book of poetry to make it to the *New York Times* best-seller list. When asked why she had turned from music to poetry, Jewel said, "If you want the most honest glimpse of me, look at my poetry. I don't exist unless I'm writing. I don't understand daylight or lovers or the world. I need it to deal with hardships in my life. There isn't a day that I can really go without it. Through it, I came to know myself."

Through *A Night Without Armor* Jewel's fans also came to know her. Jewel has admitted that the poems are the musings of an adolescent girl. "I wanted to do something that would let kids know who I am, and what I thought about when I was growing up," says Jewel. "Even though the first stuff I wrote wasn't great, it shows a process I went through—being disillusioned by love, coming to terms with my sexuality. That way, kids can go, 'Wow, she was just as confused as I am!'" Although there are poems

Jewel and Lilith Fair headliner Sarah McLachlan share a light moment. Jewel enjoyed the camaraderie of the all-female concert tour, which in addition to herself and McLachlan included such stars as Sheryl Crow, Paula Cole, and Meredith Brooks.

with such titles as "Infatuation" and "The Inertia of a Lonely Heart," there are also poems that hint at something deeper than adolescent puppy love. One poem, titled "I Say to You Idols," is a direct challenge to Jewel's pop-culture peers to be proponents of a positive outlook on life. There are also musings that amount to postcards from the road, outlining how Jewel was dealing with the stressful touring schedule that made her a star.

Most people might rest on their laurels for a bit after producing a hot-selling album and a best-seller. But not Jewel. Instead, she responded in a very odd way: she claimed she was bored! "I've become very bored with music," she said. "I've always done lots of things: sculpture, marble carving, dance. I've devoted four years of my life to music, but I reached a point where it was no longer a challenge. I was dying of boredom." At first Jewel's fans were shocked by that statement. The Internet chat rooms were full of speculation: What would she do? Would she give up singing altogether? As things turned out, the change wasn't quite so drastic.

It shouldn't have come as a surprise that, like pop superstars Madonna and Whitney Houston, Jewel was branching out into movies. She landed a starring role in a drama about the American Civil War that was being directed by Oscar winner Ang Lee, the director of such period movies as *Sense and Sensibility* and *The Ice Storm*. Asked about his unproven female lead's acting ability, Lee said, "Hiring Jewel was a risk-taking experience, but very rewarding. I think people are going to be very happy with her work."

The movie, titled *Ride with the Devil,* opened in November 1998 to critical, if not commercial, success. Set in Missouri during the Civil War, the movie stars Tobey Maguire and Skeet Ulrich as Jake Roedel and Jack Bull Chiles, respectively. Roedel and Chiles are Confederate army bushwhackers who conduct daring raids on enemy locations. Jewel portrays Sue Lee Shelley, a young widow who, as the war progresses, takes care of the wounded and feeds the bushwhackers.

Lee's decision to cast Jewel in the role of Sue Lee was based on how the filmmaker thought the musician would measure up against her counterparts. Lee said Jewel had "a sexual dominance that would let her hold her own with all these young men."

A review of the movie in the *New York Times* described Jewel's acting as demonstrating "low-key credibility . . . that conveys an orneriness and tough humor beneath a facade of 19th-century decorum." How did Jewel feel about the challenges of making her first movie? In typical Jewel fashion she says, "I had to relearn how to walk, to

Jewel, with Skeet Ulrich, in a scene from the film Ride with the Devil.

talk, to get rid of all my modern mannerisms. I had to realize that my face would be 20 feet tall on the screen and that a little would go a long way."

Of course, there was still the matter of Jewel's sophomore musical effort, the delayed second album. It was finally released in November of 1998, a little more than two years after the initial tracks had been recorded in the studio near Woodstock. Part of the reason for the delay was Jewel's hectic work schedule. According to the singer, "I went right from touring to the movie and the book to the album with no break. I have wanted to have a break but I keep having things I want to do." This sort of work ethic has earned her the title of hardest-working woman in pop music.

Ironically, none of the songs recorded at Bearsville appeared on the second album. Everyone involved in the album agreed on this course of action, feeling that during the interval Jewel had grown from the still-struggling folksinger into an international star. No longer an unsure teenager, but rather a confident, self-assured young woman, she wanted her second album to reflect her growth. In fact, by the time the second album, titled *Spirit,* was ready to be released, Jewel had become a bit self-conscious about her initial effort on *Pieces of You.* "I just can't listen to my singing on that record," she confesses. "I mean, it's a good record for a teenager—it's honest, it's awkward, it's all there—but having it taken so seriously was like having a student's artwork taken seriously. Student art isn't meant to be critiqued."

Her second album, although a huge hit with her fans, received the same lukewarm response from the critics as her first album. It wasn't that the record was bad, according to a review in *Rolling Stone,* but it did "a poor job of showing off Jewel's star quality, displaying none of her chutzpah, charm or humor." Jewel just couldn't seem to get a break from the music critics. Her first album was ridiculed as being nothing more than the confessions of an adolescent girl. But when she tried to show her grown-up side, she was criticized for not putting out the confessions of an adolescent girl. Once again early sales were sluggish. But by the spring of 2000, *Spirit* had joined its predecessor as a triple-platinum-selling album. Like the tortoise in the fable of the tortoise and the hare, Jewel may not have started quick off the line, but she ended up winning the race.

Jewel doesn't seem very concerned about her harsh treatment from the critics. She continues to write, play her guitar, and plan for the future. The one aspect of her personality that has served her well throughout her rise to fame is her confidence and belief in herself and her mission. It has helped her keep herself on an even keel, whether she's confronted with criticism or praise. "I think I'd be foolhardy to believe in [my popularity] too much," she said in a 1999 interview. "I'm still wet behind the ears, I'm just learning. I want to get better. It would be preposterous to say at my age I'm very good at my craft. I feel like I'm just getting my tricks down." Her Everyday Angels, and the rest of the music world, could be in for a real treat when she finally learns those tricks.

Jewel has always viewed her music as a means of uplifting other people, and a concern for social issues continues to guide her life. In 1999 she and her mother established a nonprofit organization, Higher Ground for Humanity, to promote various environmental and humanitarian efforts.

7

HIGHER GROUND

THE STORY OF JEWEL'S RISE to stardom in the entertainment industry is almost too good to be true. Growing up as far from the world of glitz and glamour as one can get, she still managed to conquer it. Of course, plenty of work has gone into her success. And she has carefully avoided the pitfalls that success can bring.

Despite a high-profile fling with actor Sean Penn, Jewel has been one of the few celebrities in recent years to remain mostly out of the gossip columns. There could be any number of reasons for this, but the main reason may be her refusal to view herself as anything other than simply Jewel Kilcher from Homer, Alaska. Even though fame came to her at a young age, she has had the wisdom to stay away from its dark side. "I see why it destroys a lot of people," she says. "I have incredible people around me who know my goals spiritually. I also knew why I got into music—to help people. I've never had to compromise my integrity. I've never worried about being cool or hip. It's allowed me to remain sane."

Her friendships with people like Steve Poltz and Sean Penn have helped keep her grounded. Poltz is a talented musician who has never cared about the spotlight, and Penn has had his own problems with celebrity. From these two distinctly different men she has learned not to take herself too seriously, and that fame is a natural result of talent. Although she's been linked with some very high-profile celebrities, she isn't ready to settle down anytime soon, in part because her music and her spiritual growth come first. "I spent a lot of my life alone, which isn't sad to me," she says. "I move emotionally a lot. I outgrow things quickly. I'm more committed to my growth than to staying with friends."

Perhaps boyfriends have tended to come and go quickly in Jewel's life, but one man has had an enduring influence on Jewel, preparing her to handle the sudden adoration of her fans and the media: her father, Atz. Although there have been hard times, such as her parents' divorce, Jewel has always remained close to the man from whom she learned so much. From the early years when Jewel, barely out of diapers, joined the family singing troupe at county fairs, to the lonely times when she played to sparse crowds while promoting her first album, Jewel has kept close to her heart the lessons she learned from Atz. It isn't just the music, though. Jewel says that her upbringing on the farm, and specifically the discipline required to make a farm run smoothly, helped prepare her for the hard work of touring. "It kept me sane," she says.

Of course, it isn't just the men in her life that have helped her deal with her success. She wouldn't have even attempted to pursue her dream had it not been for the faith, love, and support of her mother. More than just encouraging her daughter to become a pop musician, Nedra encouraged Jewel to pursue her dreams and do what she needed to take care of her spirit. It's really this focus on doing what's good for her spirit that sets Jewel apart from her performing peers and keeps her out of the gossip columns. Jewel doesn't tour so much to promote her records, or for fame or money. She does it, she says, because "it serves my spirit and reminds people to live their dreams."

Even though to an outsider it may seem that Jewel is promoting a record or herself, she's really promoting her philosophy of personal sincerity and honesty. "[I] never found satisfaction in parties or bars or getting compliments from people who didn't know me," she said. "I need substance and I need truth, and I find that kids are very hungry for sincerity."

An appropriate name for Jewel's philosophy might be, as she has called it, "intelligent optimism." Unlike the optimism of a Hollywood musical or a children's storybook, the optimism that Jewel speaks of takes into account that there are things we can change and things we can't. She says:

> What a lot of people call optimism is actually denial. It's a blind conservative optimism: everything's fine, there's no problem, look on the bright side. It's rubbish. There are obvious problems in the world and your experiences can make you bitter or they can make you determined to overcome. That's a choice we make, I guess, every day. Cynicism is fun, it's kind of a nice brain game because it's smart, but ultimately it doesn't help much. I look at someone like Martin Luther King who knew what tremendous opposition he faced and stayed mercilessly focused on what change was possible, because he knew that lending the problem his despair was to become part of the problem. It's something I've thought about a lot. If I [feel] poorly, or when my circumstances are poor, I want to know the quickest route to getting better. Which means working out what I am going to do, how am I contributing to the problem, how can I control at least what I can? It means getting a lot more conscious of your life and a lot more thoughtful. To me that's intelligent optimism, and that's what I choose. Cynicism isn't smarter, it's just safer.

On a personal level, when Jewel found herself living in San Diego, going from one dead-end, low-paying job to another, feeling the cold stares of those more fortunate, she could have become bitter and resentful. Instead she took some rather unusual steps to make her life and her world better. She quit trying to live an American dream that just wasn't working for her. She moved into her van and began making the music that one day would inspire people all over the world. Her belief in herself and her strong spirit allowed her to take the hard, high road to becoming a successful musician. It would have been easier to be a cashier at a discount store, or even to become an executive assistant answering phones all day. But Jewel had never taken the easy way out: whether she was teaching herself to yodel at age 6 or to play the guitar at 16, she knew where she wanted to go and how to get there.

After hitting it big and realizing just how much money a triple-platinum-selling album brings in, Jewel began looking for a way to put that money, and her philosophy, to practical use. The groundwork for what would become the nonprofit organization Higher Ground for Humanity actually took place before Jewel was anything other than a homeless folksinger. Jewel's basic philosophy all along had been to help raise people's spirits through her music. But once she realized that her records could also be commercially viable products, her dream of helping raise the spirits of the world took a different track.

To achieve the goals they had adopted, Jewel and Nedra launched Higher Ground for Humanity on January 21, 1999, in New York. The organization's stated mission is "to promote human excellence by pioneering what it means to be a human being in the highest sense, inspiring new possibilities for humanity." Higher Ground for Humanity works toward this mission by sponsoring or supporting its partner organizations throughout the world.

Fund-raising is not the primary focus of Higher Ground for Humanity, which seeks like-minded entrepreneurs to dedicate mainly their time and expertise to the shared goals. Instead, Higher Ground for Humanity encourages each person to actually do something to help the world. "It's an umbrella organization that coordinates programs

Jewel sings with Bono of the group U2 at a NetAid concert. Sponsored by the United Nations, the concert series was intended to bring attention to the problem of world poverty.

and provides support for a wide variety of environmental and humanitarian efforts," says Jewel. "You get more done with a united front."

Jewel has an honest and caring reason for starting Higher Ground for Humanity. "Helping people is such a trite little summary," she says. "In my own life, I've felt deeply many things, intense loneliness, intense worries for survival, and there's people that go through worse daily. It's not OK for me to just be breathing. It's not OK for me just to get by." For Jewel, dedicating her time, energy, and resources to helping other people isn't just something she thinks is a good idea. It's much more fundamental than that. "Even the arts are secondary in my life," she says. "It's my profession, sure, but it's not rocket science. In the

Nedra, whose encouragement during difficult times helped her daughter fulfill her dreams, continues to play a highly visible role in Jewel's life. Nedra did backup vocals on Jewel's Spirit *album, and she helped launch Higher Ground for Humanity.*

end, I think of myself as a humanitarian. I hope when it's all over, my fame is as a spokesman for causes."

For the present, however, Jewel continues to uplift and encourage her fans through her music. More than five years after her first album was released, she's still in the spotlight. She still appears on TV, and her songs are still getting heavy rotation on the radio. In November of 1999 a long-awaited third album was released, but this one was completely different from her first two. A collection of

Christmas music recorded and released especially for the holiday season, *Joy: A Holiday Collection* is made up almost entirely of some of the best-loved Christmas songs ever written. It includes a wide range of styles and feelings, from serious and sublime hymns such as "Silent Night" and "Hark! The Herald Angels Sing" to more popular songs such as "Rudolph the Red-Nosed Reindeer" and "Winter Wonderland." Although it didn't climb up the pop charts like her other albums, Jewel wasn't too distressed by that. "Staying pure is the hard part and I'm still learning what it takes to keep your creative spirit alive," she says. "Every record doesn't have to sell 10 million [copies]. You have to be bold and prepared to fail." Of course, almost no one who has heard the album would use the term *failure* to describe it. Instead her fans see it as simply another example of Jewel's desire to keep expanding her talent and interests beyond the usual pop music boundaries.

Indeed, Jewel is anything but a typical pop music star. Since the beginning of her career, she has remained down-to-earth. Her clothes, hair, and makeup have perhaps gotten a bit more stylish since the days of living in her van, but that's to be expected. Thrift-shop T-shirts and cutoffs may be proper attire for hanging out on the beach and writing poems, but going to the Grammys requires something a bit more formal.

Yet Jewel has been able to handle the glamorous side of fame with the same equanimity with which she handles the adoration of millions of fans. She makes it look easy to be naturally beautiful, but it wasn't always that way. As a young girl Jewel went through some of the same body-image problems that many young women face. She continues to deal with those issues, even after achieving fame and fortune. "I think I'm OK, but you know, I have days where I just don't want to go on television because I ate Ben & Jerry's last night and I can't face the world," she says.

Luckily she also knows that body size and body image

"I'm still learning what it takes to keep your creative spirit alive," Jewel has confessed. Whatever her future brings, the multifaceted artist seems committed to the goal of nurturing her spirit—and the spirits of her many fans.

are separate from talent, personality, and health. Stand Jewel next to most of the young women on TV sitcoms or any of the female teenage pop stars and the difference is noticeable. In Jewel you'll see a young woman comfortable with who she is and how her body looks. And because of her chronic kidney problems, eating the right kinds of foods and taking care of her body are very important to her. The limelight can be a tough place to try to maintain your equilibrium, though. "I'm committed to trying to be healthy . . ." says Jewel. "I'm committed to being in front of people and not being perfect."

Through all the hard times and good times, the fame, the fortune, the gossip, the grueling tour schedule—through it all Jewel has remained an open, caring, honest human being. None of the trappings of stardom have turned her faith away from believing in the goodness of humanity and the possibility of greatness that resides in all people, no matter who they are, where they live, or how much money they make. This quality, more than her talent or beauty, is what makes Jewel a star. "I want to do with my life what is worthwhile," she says. "I think in the end, kindness matters. People understanding their own beauty and divinity matters. Whatever career I'm in, it has to be toward those goals." It's this philosophy that makes Jewel's fans love her so dearly and silences her detractors.

APPENDIX

FACTS ABOUT THE HOMELESS IN AMERICA

Jewel is only one of the millions of Americans who have been homeless at one time or another. People usually become homeless for one of three reasons. First, they may be displaced from their homes by natural or man-made disasters, such as hurricanes and fires. Second, they may lose their home or possessions through family breakups, abuse, or loss of a job. Runaway or "throwaway" children and abused women and children are also included in this group. These people often have difficulty resettling permanently. The third and smallest group consists of those who are chronically homeless—that is, those who remain so for long periods of time. The people in this group are more likely to suffer from substance abuse or mental illness.

Many of us think that we know who homeless people are: male adults who are either mentally ill or have drug and alcohol problems, who don't work and don't want to, who are uneducated, or who live in major cities. In fact, according to statistics, these assumptions are true for only a fraction of America's homeless. Here are some facts about the homeless in the United States:

- The average age of a homeless person in America is nine.**
- Families with young children are the fastest-growing segment of the homeless population, making up 40% of people who become homeless.++
- Children account for about 24% of the urban homeless population.++
- The typical homeless family is a single, 20-year-old mother with one or two children under the age of six.**
- Twenty-five to 50% of homeless women and children are fleeing abuse.+
- Over half of all homeless children have never lived in their own home.
- Over 40% have been homeless more than once.**
- About 30% of homeless adults have full- or part-time jobs.* (In many areas of the country, a person who works full-time at a minimum-wage job is at risk for homelessness because his or her pay often cannot cover the cost of housing.)
- Many homeless people have completed high school; some have attended college or graduate school.*

- Forty percent of homeless men have served in the armed forces (compared to 34% of the general adult male population).+
- The ethnic makeup of homeless populations varies according to geographic location. In major cities, for example, 57% are African American, 30% are white, and 13% are Hispanic, Native American, or Asian.# In rural areas, however, most homeless people are white, and homelessness among Native Americans is more common in these areas.
- About 20 to 25% of the single adult homeless population suffers from some form of mental illness; of these, only 5 to 7% need to be institutionalized.+
- About one in four homeless people are substance abusers; of these, most are also mentally ill.*

Sources:

* The American Homeless Society, 1996
** Homes for the Homeless, 1996
\+ National Coalition for the Homeless, 1997
++ U.S. Bureau of the Census, 1991
\# U.S. Conference of Mayors Survey, 1996

ORGANIZATIONS THAT HELP THE HOMELESS

Habitat for Humanity International
121 Habitat Street
Americus, GA 31709-3498
phone: 800-422-4828
fax: 912-924-0641
E-mail: info@habitat.org

Homes for the Homeless
36 Cooper Square, 6th Floor
New York, NY 10003
phone: 212-529-5252
fax: 212-529-7698
E-mail: hn4061@handsnet.org

National Alliance to End Homelessness (formerly the Nat'l. Citizens Committee for Food & Shelter)
1518 K Street N.W., Suite 206
Washington, DC 20005
phone: 202-638-1526
fax: 202-638-4664
E-mail: naeh@ari.net

National Coalition for the Homeless
1621 K Street N.W., Suite 1004
Washington, DC 20006
phone: 202-775-1322
fax: 202-775-1316
E-mail: nch@ari.net

National Student Campaign Against Hunger & Homelessness
Julie Miles, Director
11965 Venice Boulevard, Suite 408
Los Angeles, CA 90066
phone: 800-664-8647, ext. 324
fax: 310-391-0053
E-mail: nscah@aol.com

FINDING OUT MORE ABOUT HOMELESSNESS

BOOKS:

Ackerman, Karen. *The Leaves in October*. New York: Yearling Books, 1993.

Barbour, Karen. *Mr. Bow Tie*. New York: Harcourt Brace Jovanovich, 1991.

Bunting, Eve. *Fly Away Home*. Boston: Houghton Mifflin Company, 1991.

Chalofsky, Margie, et al. *Changing Places: A Kid's View of Shelter Living*. Beltsville, MD: Gryphon House, 1992.

Clifford, Eth. *Never Hit a Ghost with a Baseball Bat*. Illustrated by George Hughes. Boston: Houghton Mifflin Company, 1993.

Disalvo-Ryan, Dyanne. *Uncle Willie and the Soup Kitchen*. New York: William Morrow & Co., Inc., 1990.

Fox, Paula. *Monkey Island*. New York: Orchard Books, 1991.

Hahn, Mary Downing. *December Stillness*. New York: Avon Books, 1988.

Hertenstein, Jane. *Home Is Where We Live: Life in a Shelter Through a Young Girl's Eyes*. Illustrated by Bonnie Lee Groth. Chicago: Cornerstone Press, 1995.

Hubbard, Jim. *Lives Turned Upside Down: Homeless Children in Their Own Words and Photographs*. New York: Simon & Schuster, 1996.

Kroll, Virginia L. *Shelter Folks*. Illustrated by Jan Naimo Jones. Grand Rapids, MI: Wm. B. Eerdmans Publishing Company, 1995.

Kroloff, Charles A. *54 Ways You Can Help the Homeless*. New York: Levin Associates, 1993.

London, Jonathan. *Where's Home?* New York: Puffin Books, 1997.

Luger, Harriett. *Bye, Bye, Bali Kai*. New York: Browndeer Press, 1996.

Mazer, Harry. *Cave Under the City*. New York: HarperCollins, 1986.

McGovern, Ann. *The Lady in the Box*. Illustrated by Marni Backer. New York: Turtle Books, 1997.

Mountbatten-Windsor York (Ferguson), Sarah. *Bright Lights*. Illustrated by Jacqueline Rogers. New York: Bantam Books, 1997.

Myers, Bill, and Robert West. *Beauty in the Least*. Wheaton, IL: Tyndale House Publishers, 1993.

Myers, Walter Dean. *Darnell Rock Reporting*. New York: Yearling Books, 1996.

Neufeld, John. *Almost a Hero*. New York: Aladdin Paperbacks, 1996.

Rozakis, Laurie. Homelessness: *Can We Solve the Problem?* Edited by Jeanne Vestal. Chicago: Twenty First Century Books, 1995.

Sendak, Maurice. *We Are All in the Dumps with Jack and Guy*. New York: HarperCollins, 1993.

Snyder, Zilpha Keatley. *The Gypsy Game*. New York: Delacorte Press, 1997.

Stewart, Gail B. *The Homeless*. San Diego: Lucent Books, 1996.

VIDEOS:

Don't Make Me Choose. Color/b & w, no date. Produced by Night Vision Productions. Music by Lorrie "Wes" Wesoly. 17 min. Night Vision Productions.

Home Less Home. Color, 1991. 70 min. Bill Brand Productions.

The Homeless Home Movie. Color, 1997. Produced and directed by Pat Hennessey. 84 min. Media Visions.

Rewind: It Could Have Been Me. B & w, no date. Produced, directed, and animated by Lorie Loeb. Music by Holly Near. 13 min. Morning Glory Films.

Survivors of the Streets: Success Stories of Four Who Were Homeless. Color, no date. Produced by Charlann Slater. 28 min. Full Circle Productions.

WEBSITES:

The American Homeless Society Presents Homeless Shelters in the United States
http://www.nmc.edu/~lanninl/us.htm

The Homeless Art Project
http://www.floaters.org/index1.html

Homeless People and the Internet
http://members.tripod.com/~bmdavidson/index.html

Homeless Peoples Network
http://aspin.asu.edu/hpn/

Kids Helping Kids
http://www.geocities.com/Heartland/8677/

North American Street Newspaper Association
http://www.speakeasy.org/nasna

CHRONOLOGY

1974 Jewel is born on May 23 to Atz Kilcher and Lenedra Carroll Kilcher in Payson, Utah

1980 At the age of six begins performing with her parents in local bars in Anchorage, Alaska

1982 Parents' divorce; Jewel and her two brothers move to the family farm in Homer, Alaska

1988 "Adopted" by Ottawa Indian tribe, an experience she credits with helping her learn to write from the heart

1989 Heard on the radio for the first time singing "Somewhere over the Rainbow"; begins playing the guitar and performing songs she wrote; is briefly part of a band called La Crème

1990 Enters Interlochen Fine Arts Academy in Michigan as a voice major in her junior year; becomes first voice major to perform in a drama

1992 Graduates from Interlochen and moves to San Diego, where her mother is living; after failing to keep several jobs, moves into a van to cut costs and pursue music

1993 Performances at the Innerchange attract the attention of record company executives; signs a record deal with Atlantic late in the year

1995 First album, *Pieces of You,* debuts; wins American Music Award for Best New Artist

1998 Second album, *Spirit,* debuts at number three on the Billboard chart; book of poetry, *A Night Without Armor,* is released

1999 *Pieces of You* becomes one of the top five best-selling albums of all time by a female artist; Jewel and her mother establish nonprofit, humanitarian organization Higher Ground for Humanity

2000 Second book, *Chasing Down the Dawn,* is released in October; it contains poetry, stories, essays, and observations

DISCOGRAPHY

1995 *Pieces of You*

1998 *Spirit*

1999 *Joy: A Holiday Collection*

PUBLISHED WORKS

1998 *A Night Without Armor: Poems* (NewYork: HarperCollins)

2000 *Chasing Down the Dawn* (New York: Harper Entertainment)

FURTHER READING

Gray, Scott. *Heart Song: The Story of Jewel.* New York: Ballantine, 1998.

Kemp, Kristen. *Jewel: Pieces of a Dream.* New York: Archway, 1998.

MacFarland, P. J. *Angel Standing By: The Story of Jewel.* New York: Griffin, 1999.

West, Tracey. *Jewel: Music's Hottest Treasure.* New York: Scholastic, 1998.

Woodworth, Marc, ed. *Solo: Women Singer-Songwriters in Their Own Words.* New York: Delta, 1998.

INDEX

INDEX

PICTURE CREDITS

Page:
2: AP/Wide World Photos
10: AP/Wide World Photos
13: AP/Wide World Photos
15: AP/Wide World Photos
16: © Steve Kaufman/Corbis
19: © Jim Rosen/Ken Graham Agency
20: © Peter Johnson/Corbis
23: © Jim Rosen/Ken Graham Agency
24: © Jim Rosen/Ken Graham Agency
26: © Judy L. Hasday
30: Courtesy Interlochen Center for the Arts
33: Bettmann/Corbis
34: Courtesy Interlochen Center for the Arts
39: © Nik Wheeler/Corbis
42: Underwood & Underwood/Corbis
44: © Marko Shark/Corbis
48: © S.I.N./Corbis
50: © Jim Rosen/Ken Graham Agency
55: AP/Wide World Photos
56: © Philip Gould/Corbis
58: © Steve Jennings/Corbis
63: © S.I.N./Corbis
64: AP/Wide World Photos
67: © Mitchell Gerber/Corbis
68: © Neal Preston/Corbis
70: AP/Wide World Photos
73: AP/Wide World Photos
75: © Sin/Colin Hawkins/Corbis
77: Photofest
80: AP/Wide World Photos
85: AP/Wide World Photos
86: © Pacha/Corbis
88: © Pacha/Corbis

Cover Photo: © Mitchel Gerber/Corbis

JOHN THOMPSON is a freelance writer currently living in Breckenridge, Texas, where he grew up. In his spare time he plays golf, listens to Mozart, and feeds his cat.

JAMES SCOTT BRADY serves on the board of trustees with the Center to Prevent Handgun Violence and is the vice chairman of the Brain Injury Foundation. Mr. Brady served as assistant to the president and White House press secretary under President Ronald Reagan. He was severely injured in an assassination attempt on the president, but remained the White House press secretary until the end of the administration. Since leaving the White House, Mr. Brady has lobbied for stronger gun laws. In November 1993, President Bill Clinton signed the Brady Bill, a national law requiring a waiting period on handgun purchases and a background check on buyers.